Team Intelligence

Also by Jon Levy

You're Invited: The Art and Science of Connection, Trust, and Belonging

The 2 AM Principle: Discover the Science of Adventure

Team Intelligence

How Brilliant Leaders Unlock Collective Genius

Jon Levy

HARPER
BUSINESS
An Imprint of HarperCollinsPublishers

Without limiting the exclusive rights of any author, contributor or the publisher of this publication, any unauthorized use of this publication to train generative artificial intelligence (AI) technologies is expressly prohibited. HarperCollins also exercise their rights under Article 4(3) of the Digital Single Market Directive 2019/790 and expressly reserve this publication from the text and data mining exception.

TEAM INTELLIGENCE. Copyright © 2025 by Jonathan Levy. All rights reserved. Printed in the United States of America. No part of this book may be used or reproduced in any manner whatsoever without written permission except in the case of brief quotations embodied in critical articles and reviews. For information, address HarperCollins Publishers, 195 Broadway, New York, NY 10007. In Europe, HarperCollins Publishers, Macken House, 39/40 Mayor Street Upper, Dublin 1, D01 C9W8, Ireland.

HarperCollins books may be purchased for educational, business, or sales promotional use. For information, please email the Special Markets Department at SPsales@harpercollins.com.

hc.com

FIRST EDITION

Image on p. 8 by Trafton Drew, *Psych Science*. All other images courtesy of the author.

Designed by Michele Cameron

Library of Congress Cataloging-in-Publication Data has been applied for.

ISBN 978-0-06-339957-0

25 26 27 28 29 LBC 5 4 3 2 1

To the gods old and new
Thank you for all that you have given me

Contents

Brilliant Leaders Start Here 1

Part I: Leadership—Unburdened

Chapter 1: Mis-Leading 21

Chapter 2: Why Should Anyone Follow You? 43

Chapter 3: Growing Your Skills 61

Part II: Teams—Unlocked

Chapter 4: Welcome to the Team 85

Chapter 5: Super Chickens (The Too-Much-Talent Problem) . . 103

Chapter 6: Team Intelligence—Reasoning 123

Chapter 7: Team Intelligence—Attention 135

Chapter 8: Team Intelligence—Resources 153

Chapter 9: The Good and the Bad 167

Part III: Organizations—Unleashed

Chapter 10: Welcome to the Corporate Family 187

Chapter 11: Becoming the Leader We Need 211

Acknowledgments 223
Notes 225
Index 237

Team Intelligence

Brilliant Leaders Start Here

It was the peak of the Cold War, and the International Olympic Committee had selected Moscow for the 1980 Summer Games. As the leader of the free world, President Jimmy Carter had made a difficult decision. He would not legitimize the Soviet Union by sending athletes to represent the US in the capital of communism.

His decision had a profound impact on the hundreds of Olympic hopefuls who had sacrificed so much for their chance to earn Olympic glory. Imagine being nineteen years old and having trained since childhood for a once-in-a-lifetime opportunity to represent your country and then having that taken away from you.

Among these hopefuls was the US national basketball team, at the time made up of college-aged student-athletes. Although the boycott of communism was disappointing and frustrating for everyone, capitalism was able to swoop in and save the day. The NBA would sell tickets to five exhibition games between the NBA All-Star Team and Team USA. The favored team was obviously the NBA All-Stars. They were the best and most seasoned players, in the prime of their careers, and they were coached by Lenny Wilkens, whose Seattle SuperSonics had just won the 1979 NBA Championship. Meanwhile, Team USA was made up of a bunch of kids who, in between practice, needed to get to math class, budget their weekly meal plan, and avoid another argument with their roommate who didn't believe in showering.

And yet it wasn't even close. Team USA, the youngest national team ever, demolished the NBA All-Stars. In one game the Olympic team beat the All-Stars by 31 points (97–66). You might be thinking, "Well, anyone can have an off day—maybe it was a fluke." True, but in this five-game series, Team USA won 4 out of 5 games and only lost that one game by 2 points.

You might say, "Jon, Team USA was filled with talented college players, several of whom would go on to become NBA All-Stars themselves. It's not such a surprise." This is also true. Having skill is a bare minimum. The NBA All-Stars aren't going to lose to a group of potato farmers who have never picked up a ball before. Skill is the price of entry to participate, but it just isn't sufficient to win. Tons of sports teams and businesses have superstar talent and leaders, but talent alone doesn't guarantee success.

If packing in stars were enough, the US would win every Olympic basketball game. In 2004, even with an Olympic team that included legends of the game like LeBron James, Dwyane Wade, Carmelo Anthony, and Allen Iverson, they barely earned a bronze to make it on the podium. In one devastating game, they lost by 19 points to Puerto Rico. Don't get me wrong, Puerto Rico is an amazing place, but I'd never heard of their basketball team.

So, what actually makes a team effective? For too long we have been fed the narrative that success is simple: hire stars, put a star leader in charge, and let it rip.

Yet . . . the facts tell a different story. Team USA from 1980 had objectively less talent, less experience, and less time to dedicate to the sport, but they consistently beat the NBA All-Stars. It wasn't a one-time fluke. We see this kind of pattern play out across sports and business constantly. We all know the stories of inexperienced talent coming together and forming great teams, teams that are more than the sum of their parts. Countless books, articles, and documentaries have shared how Netflix took over the movie rental industry to beat out blockbusters and create streaming television as we know it, how Khan Academy displaced the textbook market by offering a better way to learn, how Airbnb disrupted the hotel industry, how unheard-of film studios like Marvel and Pixar shook up Hollywood and won big at the box office. They all lacked industry experience and traditional top-tier talent when they started but left their mark on our society. Something special was happening that allowed them to outperform their peers.

We've also heard stories of star teams coming together in business and expecting huge success only to see tragic failure. Even with former chairman of Disney Jeffrey Katzenberg and former eBay and HP CEO Meg Whitman at the helm, short-form video platform Quibi lost nearly $2 billion and had to shutter immediately after launching because this seasoned team ignored ideas that challenged their assumptions. In 1998, when car manufacturers Daimler-Benz and Chrysler came together in what was the largest merger of its kind in history, Wall Street rejoiced for the new DaimlerChrysler, but within months, the two companies combined were worth less than Daimler-Benz was on its own before the merger. Billions in value were lost because the leadership of the two companies couldn't create alignment across their missions. The cultural conflicts served as distraction and frustration, making everyone less productive. We see the trend play out across countless companies filled with incredibly talented people. From the train wreck of the AOL–Time Warner merger to the failures of Google Glass, Nokia, Yahoo, Crystal Pepsi, and Magic Leap—all had star talent on the team but just couldn't make it work.

So, what is it that separates the leaders and teams that succeed from those that fail? It all comes down to intelligence—just not the kind of IQ testing you typically hear about. Let me explain.

When we describe a person who is effective at problem-solving, we say they are intelligent. But as we have seen, taking a bunch of intelligent or talented people and putting them on a team doesn't make the team great at winning or problem-solving. You could end up with a group of smart jerks who can't work together.

When I talk about intelligence in the pages that follow, I'm talking about the skills, attitudes, and habits that help leaders and teams become smarter and more effective *together*—to be better together than they ever would be on their own. This is team intelligence. We think we need to get the smartest people in the room, but the research shows it's about creating a room where people can be their smartest together. It's not about IQ or prestigious degrees, but about what allows you to unlock the collective genius of your team. No matter where we sit in the team, we want to maximize the team's intelligence, so that we accomplish our goals or solve problems as quickly as possible with the resources we have.

You have probably listened to countless podcasts and read a library's worth of books on how to be successful. Some of them may have been fantastic, but considering there are 15,000 self-help books published *each year*, chances are that many of those aren't that great. I wish I could say that the ones written by famous executives are better. Unfortunately, you probably noticed that a lot of those authors tell us that if we were only more like them, and knew what they knew, we could have their fabulous lives. Um, I guess?

Well, actually, we don't need to guess, because in recent years, new research has helped debunk a lot of these myths. The image we have been sold by celebrity CEOs that leaders are charismatic extroverts born with essential traits that let them overcome all odds to succeed is total BS. The evidence often shows just the opposite. Many of the most successful leaders are introverted, with skills learned on the job, and a lot are flat-out awkward, which is good news for me if I want a shot at leading. It turns out there is only one universal characteristic you need to be a leader, but we will get into that in Chapter 2.

We have also been convinced that the best teams have to bond and love each other. The reality is that mutual respect and healthy habits are a lot more important than holding hands, trust falls, and singing songs like members of a seventies commune. In fact, many of the most effective teams argue constantly (but respectfully), and in the process uncover problems and improve their solutions. Is there a predictor of effective teams? Absolutely, but you'll have to wait until Chapter 7 to hear more about that. The number of myths is endless but now we finally have the research to show what makes leaders, teams, and organizations successful.

Secret Origins

Before we get into things, we are going to take a quick detour so I can share the origin story of this book. In my late twenties I wasn't having the success I hoped for, but I had a crazy idea. Researchers have shown that people's habits and actions are contagious between friends. That explains why, for a period of time in the 2000s, when my roommate started wearing those ridiculously oversize parachute pants with the useless strings that dangle, so did I. Don't judge: I bet if I looked at some old photos of you, they would be equally embarrassing. We are all influenced by our friends—and not just a little bit. For example, if you have a friend who is obese, your chances of also being obese increase by 45 percent, your friends' chances by 20 percent, and their friends' (people you have never met) by 5 percent. This kind of effect is true for smoking, voting, marriage/divorce rates, etc. So, I thought, maybe I could improve my life by creating deep and meaningful relationships with the most accomplished people in our culture. Once I connected with them, and they trusted me, then I could learn from them and gain their habits.

I was able to convince strangers to come to my home, cook me dinner, wash my dishes, and clean my floors. Oddly, they thanked me for the experience. I know this sounds very strange, so let me explain. Being a behavioral scientist and having a deep knowledge of research has its advantages. I was able to design an experience that would appeal to people and get them to connect not just with me but with each other. For more than fifteen years, I have invited groups of twelve for dinner, but there is a twist. Not only do they have to cook the meal, but they can't talk about their careers. Other than sharing their first names, the experience is anonymous. Only once the cooking is done and we sit to eat do we discover that our new friends are astronauts, Olympic medalists, C-suite of the Fortune 500, Nobel laureates, celebrities, musicians, prime ministers, and even the voice of the barking dog from the hit song "Who Let the Dogs Out" (Fun fact:

that guy won a Grammy for barking.) I don't know about you, but when I learn about strange successes like that, all I can think is that I should have made some very different choices in my life.

People hear about the dinners and imagine a meal of fancy food like foie gras or lobster, but honestly, the food at these dinners is terrible! I mean just awful. There is no Nobel Prize or Olympic medal for cooking, and even when one guest is a famous chef, it doesn't make up for eleven people who don't know how to cook. A journalist once said, "I was expecting a phenomenal meal and decent company, I got the opposite." And that's still true. After more than fifteen years, four hundred dinners (that's more than a year's worth of horrible meals), and well over 3,500 guests, it has grown into the largest community of its type around the world. The people continue to be phenomenal and the food is still mediocre.

But, thanks to that awful food, I have met and learned from the best in every field, from famous CEOs and the former leaders of the International Space Station to Olympic team captains and, yes, even the guy who barked. Every one of them is a world-class superstar in their field or who leads incredible organizations. I had the privilege of getting coaching from many of the top experts in the world, and talking to them was invaluable because, as you will see in Chapter 3, getting personal coaching from someone who is an expert can open your eyes to things you didn't see before.

But interacting with them also revealed a big problem. The more of these extraordinary leaders I met, the more I saw how different they were from each other. There didn't seem to be any consistent set of skills that stood out across them. You may have noticed the same thing about the leaders you admire, and even your leadership style versus your colleagues'. You all might be effective—just not in the same ways. Some are soft-spoken and methodical, others are loud and abrasive, and then others are visionary but humble. In fact, it's often their differences that stand out as their greatest skills. This realization had me question everything we have been taught about what makes leaders and organizations succeed. I looked at all the trainings offered in the Ivy League MBA programs, all the lists of essential leadership characteristics touted by companies and educational programs, and none of them lined up or had much common ground. Some lists include being courageous, visionary, confident, and showing gratitude, while other lists emphasize being steadfast, humble, resilient, and respectful. If what we need to be a successful leader is to be masterful at all of these things, no one would ever be able to lead a team or start a company.

Amusingly, many of these lists are the opposite characteristics of the most famous business leaders of our time. Is Elon Musk or Larry Ellison known for being humble? Was Steve Jobs? Check out some of Elon's tweets and tell me how respectful he is. So, not only do many of these lists of skills conflict with each other, but they conflict with the traits that have been proven to produce results in some of the most effective leaders in modern history. Also, if I'm honest, I have many character flaws, and spending more time trying to learn to be humble is a waste of time. If I haven't figured out how to tone down how amazing I am by now, it's just not going to happen.

Rather than beating myself up for not having some "essential" skill that isn't actually needed and isn't a fit for my personality, I wanted to understand what would get my team or organization to be more effective and work better together. After all, a leader's job is to help their people produce, so let's answer this question: How do teams operate at their best and what influence can you have as a leader?

This book aims to separate the total BS from what is actually important and effective. I will strip away all the corporate-speak, the stupid hacks and ideas that actually waste our time or, worse, make us feel inadequate for not living up to some fake ideal, and leave you with a few core principles you can apply both as a leader and as a team member. In these pages, I offer you the chance to change your perspective on what leaders do and what kind of leader and team member you can be. Most books focus on muscle-building; they tell the reader about a habit and expect the reader to repeat it over and over again, like going to the gym. The truth is no one does any exercises in books. The other approach attempts to change perspectives. Once you realize something doesn't work, you will hopefully stop wasting your time doing those things. My goal is to train your attention on a different set of skills as a leader—because for too long, you've been asked to do things that don't matter or, unfortunately, can be harmful.

Focusing on What Matters

So, let's have some fun. We begin this journey with the human lung—specifically, this scan of a human chest. Radiologists review them looking for infections, damage, cancer, etc. Take a look:

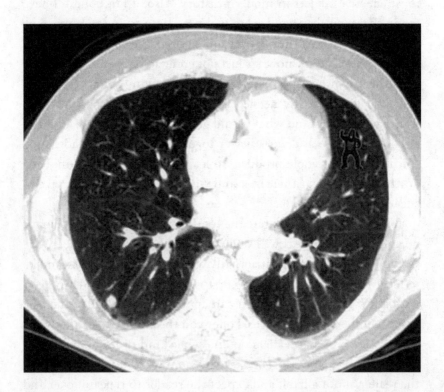

Now ask yourself: Did you notice a concerning mass? Look again.

Did you see a gorilla on the top right lung? Some people notice it, but here is what's surprising about this little game: when researchers Trafton Drew, Melissa Võ, and Jeremy Wolfe tested radiologists with this image, only 17 percent of them saw it. Think about this: 83 percent of medical professionals whose job it is to find problems in these scans don't notice the giant gorilla. That would be like an Uber driver not noticing their passenger was a giraffe, or my copy editor not catching glarings mistakes in in my boOk.*

The reason we miss the gorilla is also the reason so many things are being done wrong in the corporate world. It's what researchers Arien Mack and Irvin Rock call inattentional blindness. It is when we don't see something unexpected that is in plain sight, even though there is nothing wrong with our vision. You might think that being an expert would mean that we would notice more, but we would have to know to look for it.

Since there is way too much information coming at us at every moment, our brains are only good at noticing what we have been taught to look for. Everything else gets filtered out. Because radiologists are taught to find things like infections or cancer, they don't see the gorilla. Similarly, if I ask you to look around the room you are in for everything that is red, you won't notice everything that is blue. Paying attention to everything is impossible for the limited capacity of our brains.

But here is the important part: once you see the gorilla, you can't unsee it. These are the kinds of ideas we will explore in the coming chapters, ones that fundamentally change the way you view leadership, how teams work, and how organizations function at their best.

---

* I would like to apologize to you for the two uncorrected errors in this book. The person who missed them has been blacklisted. Moving forward, you can expect correct gramers and spelzing. I mean moving forward starting now.

Once you see why what we have been doing doesn't work, it will be hard to pretend and keep doing things that don't work.

Let me give you another example. One of the most pervasive myths in our culture is that if we want to have amazing results, we need star talent. We are obsessed with star talent. Sports teams fight for draft picks and free agents get millions of dollars to play. You may have traded your entire week's allowance and your lunch for a Pikachu Pokémon card. Meanwhile, businesses stake their futures on star leadership, and when these business leaders become famous enough, we try to emulate their styles. In the entertainment industry, star-studded blockbusters are seen by millions and make the studios fortunes. We put up posters of these people, quote them, and even line up for hours for a chance to speak to them, or in my case cook terrible food with them. All of this is done because deep down, we believe that if we lived life like them, or if they were part of our team, we would succeed. Trying to reproduce star success is how organizations end up with long lists of qualities they want their leaders to have.

The problem is that if star leadership and talent caused success, then every movie with a famous writer/director and some celebrities would be a hit, and we all know there are plenty of flops. (I was going to share a list of some, but none of us saw them anyway so there was no point.) The same is true for sports. Think back to the story of those 1980s NBA All-Stars losing to a bunch of kids on Team USA, or the 2004 US Olympic team losing to Puerto Rico and getting a bronze.

The corporate world loves the star talent narrative, and it believes in it so much that it is willing to bet really big. They take a person who checks off all the right boxes, often someone with a larger-than-life personality and an alpha attitude, and put them in charge, believing everything will work out. But we have seen how that plays out. Superstar CEOs are brought in or promoted from within to grow a company; they are given massive compensation, and—this will shock you—they often leave the organization worse off a few years later. Consider these infamous cases:

- Merrill Lynch's CEO Stan O'Neal destroyed their famously supportive company culture with his abrasive style, and because of his risky bets, he led the company into the biggest quarterly loss in its ninety-three-year history. Within a year of being forced out, the company had to be saved by Bank of America. But don't worry: Stan still walked out with $161.5 million in severance. Not bad for destroying a company and countless people's careers.

- In 2006, when Viacom's Tom Freston left the company after his impressive nine-month tenure, he must have been kicking himself for getting a meager $100 million payout.

- The CEO of Pfizer, Hank McKinnell, was fired in July 2005 because of incredible losses at the company. You will be relieved to know that even though the company was suffering, he was able to live modestly and scrape by on the $200 million in severance he received.

Wow! There isn't a person reading this that would say no to those compensation deals. If I could negotiate contracts like that, I would be able to afford good food cooked by competent people. If leaders really do bring that much value to a company, grow an organization, and provide people with a product or a service that has value, maybe they do deserve it. I don't know how to judge these things. There is no doubt that a strong leader can have an incredible impact, but what's clear is that the success of a team or organization hinges on more than one person. Superstar leaders alone aren't enough. At a certain point, team dynamics matter more than individual skills.

Of course, if you are Serena Williams, arguably the greatest tennis player of all time, you can dominate the court for more than a quarter century. When you don't need to rely on anyone but yourself during the game, singular superstar talent can be enough. But even in Serena's case, she has a team that helps her train, recover, review strategy, have the right nutrition, etc.

The reality is that almost everything worth doing requires a team, and as the team grows, the star's impact gets diluted. The skills required to win shift from shooting our shots to passing information (or a ball), communicating, strategizing, meeting, managing egos, and having to understand each other's styles. As the team grows, we often need to shift our concern from the best player to the worst and give our attention to the way we all interact. You could be the greatest pitchperson in corporate history, but if you have one incompetent teammate who accidentally deletes the presentation or makes clients uncomfortable, your pitch will fail. By the time you get to the size of five players on a basketball court, talent is still very important, but only if everyone is competent and can work together. When you get to the level of a large organization, competence, culture, and company dynamics matter even more.

This is where the corporate world gets confused. People believe that with a star leader, the team or the organization will align. When we are honest, we know that doesn't usually work, and that's because the essential unit of productivity is not a leader or an individual but a team. All you need is one jerk to ruin the game.

Going Beyond the Leader

Globally companies spend about $390–550 billion on training a year. A lot of that is very useful. If you need to use a hazmat suit at work, and you don't know how, training can keep you safe. Contrary to what comic books have taught us, the side effects of radiation exposure aren't superpowers, they are medical problems like lymphoma. Proper training is the difference between a long healthy career and contracting Ebola or inhaling toxic chemicals. About $40 billion is spent on leadership training, and here is my favorite part: according to leadership research by Barbara Kellerman there is no evidence that almost any of it has a long-term impact on leadership performance. And why would it? In a two-day leadership course at some Holiday Inn Express, the instructors can't account for the complexity of people. How could someone learn to handle every scenario and practice it enough to be competent or form new habits in such a short time? On the bright side, a person can become overconfident in a skill that they learned five minutes before and not see their shortcomings until it's too late.

Imagine your leader took a course over the weekend. On Monday they walk in, and you and the rest of the team have no idea you are about to be part of a leader flexing their new skill—let's say, how to give better feedback, or how to lead better meetings. Chances are they will be trying out their new skill and something unexpected will happen, but rather than this being a learning opportunity, the leader will try to save face and revert to the way they did things before. The real world is complex, and leaders deal with all the different versions of what it looks like when people have bad days. It's the same reason almost no one sticks with their diet. It's also why, after a year of Duolingo Spanish lessons, I can barely order a "cerveza" when I go with my friends to the "bibliotheca"—wait, is that bar or library? Whichever it is, creating new habits and developing skills clearly takes time, practice, and ongoing opportunities to test those skills. I'm not saying we shouldn't do any training at all, but instead, we should have fair expectations. It takes years to develop these skills, and if we are honest, it may not be worth it. It might be simpler to hire someone on the team who has the skills we don't.

I interviewed countless corporate executives from the Fortune 500, and when I shared this research and the reasoning, *none* of them were surprised. They all knew, but they were stuck because companies need "leadership training" to make star talent feel special and give them an opportunity to connect with each other and more senior executives. This is how they retain their superstars. And they need to do that because the smallest unit of productivity is not a leader or manager, but a team.

This brings us back to the big question we are trying to tackle: How do leaders maximize a team's intelligence? One of the most important lessons I have learned as a behavioral scientist is that just about everything we do to produce results, we do backward. When it comes to business success, we are focused on the wrong side of the problem. The way to make you more successful won't come from traditional leadership training. Instead, it comes from understanding how teams operate and how to affect team dynamics. If I train a leader to lead their nine-person team, even if it did work (and we know it doesn't), it will affect nine one-directional relationships (from the leader to their reports). Instead, if we do it backward and focus on the team dynamics for all ten team members, then we strengthen forty-five two-directional relationships (from each team member to their colleagues and back). Take a look at the figure below to see what I mean:

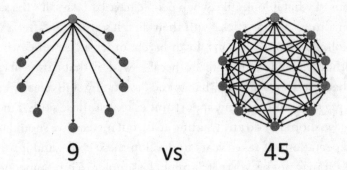

9 VS 45

Most of the work a team does is not directly with the leader; instead, the magic happens in dynamics *between* team members. An effective leader's job is to accomplish goals by getting the team to operate at its best. This means maximizing team intelligence.

This is the paradox of success: focusing on creating teams that operate well is what makes an effective leader, but focusing purely on the leader does almost nothing for the team. It makes me wonder why companies have leadership training and management training, but almost no team training outside of the military.

You are hopefully beginning to notice two things. The first is that we have the entire premise of leadership backward, and the second is that we are equally confused about our roles on teams. Put simply, no matter where we sit in an org chart, our job is to have the team succeed, but we rarely focus on the habits and ideas that unlock team intelligence.

So where do we go from here? Well, we will most certainly be poking holes in more stupid ideas, and may disrupt another industry or five, but first, we need to start by understanding how we got here. If we are going to be great leaders and team members, we should understand who we are, what about leadership development doesn't work, what does, and then, most importantly, how to create effective intelligent teams regardless of our role in the group or organization.

We have now reached the mandatory part of a business book where I entice you into reading the whole thing by promising big insights and leaving you wondering how to accomplish them. Throughout this book we will explore three major areas:

1. *Leadership—Unburdened:* What makes a great leader? Think about it like this . . . Take any leadership trait you have been told is important, and you will find countless celebrity CEOs who act the opposite and still succeed. Does that mean that nothing matters? Of course not. That wouldn't make sense either. Something has to be useful, but what? As strange as it sounds, we will look to a wolf researcher who accidentally defined our attitude toward leadership, a test that can judge if you are fit for the job, visit with Mother Teresa to discover what made her so effective, and meet a man who led a revolution in mathematics but didn't even know how to boil water or do his laundry. In the process we will break apart all the misguided ideas we

have been convinced are true about leadership, learn what useless habits have burdened us and held us back, and answer the timeless question of what makes someone a great leader. As an added bonus, we will emphasize what you should focus on if you want to stand out as part of your team. (Fun fact: it's probably not what you have been told to improve on.)

2. *Teams—Unlocked:* Think you know what makes a great team? So did I before I researched this book. We will enter the world of super chickens, elite hens that lay more eggs than any other, to learn what makes them productive, and in the process learn how Team USA from 1980 beat the NBA All Stars. We then visit the most elite fighter pilots in the world, the heist of the century, and even little plastic bricks to understand the three pillars of team intelligence (Reasoning, Attention, and Resources) and how they work so you can unlock the collective genius of your team. We will learn about people who could multiply your team's success from the moment they join and the right way to leverage the strength of superstars. As we challenge the ideas of team performance, you will discover what role you can play to make the team succeed. Every leader wants their team to be more than the sum of their parts; we now know what you can do to make it happen.

3. *Organizations—Unleashed:* Chances are your team is part of an organization, so how do we maximize our team's effectiveness while maneuvering the complexities of the whole company? As if that's not challenging enough, so much has changed in the last few years, and it's difficult to know how to have your team operate in the modern workplace when the people we work with may be distributed around the world. Moving forward, how do

we unleash the potential of our organizations, our teams, and ourselves? And what can we learn from an American World War II bomb defuser about how to navigate all these complexities? As we explore these questions, we will give definitive research-based answers and perspectives that will make you, your team, and your organization more effective.

At this point, I hope I've made you curious and left you with so many unanswered questions that you can't wait to turn the page. (Even if I didn't, you should turn the page now.)

Part I

Leadership—Unburdened

Chapter 1

Mis-Leading

If we want to accomplish anything significant, we can't do it alone. Even the top tennis players, chess prodigies, and scientific minds build teams of collaborators, mentors, and coaches that increase their effectiveness. Unless your greatest aspirations are to sit at home alone watching TV or to be a hermit in a tinfoil hat hiding in the woods, we need other people, and that means at some point you are going to need to lead something. It could be a global organization with billions in revenue, your family through a tough time, the local parent-teacher association, or a group activity at work. Some of us rise to positions of leadership, while others have leadership thrust upon us because the people above us are too incompetent to do it themselves. The point is, we can't avoid it, so we'd better understand what works.

I know you are reading this hoping for a simple answer, but any great business book (and many terrible ones) will first show you how wrong and downright stupid everything we currently believe is. Here's why: if we don't clear out bad ideas first, they will taint the good ones. It would be like inviting your toxic ex to your wedding—they are bound to cause problems. So, let's start with poking fun at what we have been taught about leadership.

The Alpha Mentality

Popular media loves to portray leaders as having strength and conviction. If anyone gets in their way, a great leader will dominate their opponent and ensure success. People with these personalities are often called "alpha." A 2004 *Harvard Business Review* article titled "Coaching the Alpha Male" begins by saying, "Highly intelligent, confident, and successful, alpha males represent about 70% of all senior executives. As the label implies, they're the people who aren't happy unless they're the top dogs—the ones calling the shots."

It's no surprise that 70 percent of all senior executives are alphas. In nature, the strongest and most dominant members control the group and ensure it thrives. It explains the popularity of shows like *Succession* or even *Yellowstone*, where the lead characters fight for dominance, and vulnerability is viewed as a weakness. Whoever is in control wins, and that is the team that we want to be on, and the leader we want to have. If we are not winning, it simply means we are not alpha enough.

But we should ask, where did this idea of the pack leader come from? Why do we believe we are in a dog-eat-dog world?

In 1970, L. David Mech had become an unexpected superstar. This soft-spoken and gentle animal researcher had just published his book *The Wolf*. I'll let you guess what it's about. In the book, Mech shared impressive research, including describing that wolf packs are led by alpha males, who maintain control through domination and intimidation. The idea spread through popular culture and was eaten up by the business world, especially by all those who loved to control and intimidate. We saw this attitude popularized over the next decades, with characters like Gordon Gekko in the movie *Wall Street* or Tony Montana from *Scarface*, or even in more recent shows like *Billions*. But there were two big problems with this analogy. The first should be obvious: What does it matter how wolves behave? We aren't wolves—we are humans living in a rapidly developing culture. Wolves lick themselves clean in public. Does that mean that, mid–board meeting, the CEO should pause to self-groom? Wolves also don't know how to operate industrial machinery or download a PDF. Does that mean your boss shouldn't either? Well, actually, your boss often can't do those things. But the point is, wolf behavior doesn't define human behavior.

The bigger problem for Mech was that when he continued his research in the 1990s he realized he was wrong. He found that when wolves reach mating age, they tend to break off from the pack and find a mating pair. The two start their own pack made up of them and their cubs. The reason it previously looked so much like domination is that researchers saw the parents guiding their young, and young wolves can be big. If your kid was misbehaving in public and you yelled at them, it would look like you were leading through domination as well. Are there times when wolf packs merge and there are battles for control? Sure, but it's not all about control; it's about teaching their cubs to survive and keeping them safe in the process.

In fact, in interviews with wolf researchers and caretakers, they shared what should have been an obvious point: Overly aggressive pack leaders can get into unnecessary fights that lead to injury and casualties. This weakens the pack. If the pack leaders are too dominant, the pack members are likely to leave or remove their leader.

So now ask yourself, if you were forced to do business with someone who was constantly trying to dominate you, would you want to interact with them? Of course not. The concept of an alpha leader is a complete lie. For starters, it depends on the context. You might have the most status at the company you started but when you go in for a surgical procedure, you are best off if the lead surgeon is in charge. Each culture has its own status system, and no one can dominate them all.

More importantly, most executives you will meet aren't dominant, and they aren't unhappy because they aren't "top dogs." Are there some? Of course, but chances are most of the ones you could name are from TV shows or movies because their outsize personalities make for great entertainment.

So, what about these dominant personalities we keep hearing about? It's important to realize two things. The first is that we tend to become aware of leaders when they are profiled by the media, and these outlets make money the more people look at their content, so media outlets are incentivized to cover sensational stories. When given the option between covering the average CEO and someone who causes a spectacle, who do you think is going to get attention? It's an unofficial game some CEOs play with journalists. If you say or do something controversial, we will write about you, and that attention can boost your stock value, so you are more successful. It doesn't mean their product is any better, or that they are better leaders; it just means they are good at playing the media game.

If you have ever had the absolute displeasure of flying ultralow-cost Irish airline Ryanair, it might be because of the CEO's knack for getting attention. On Ryanair, you can fly for absurdly low prices—United Kingdom to Hungary for $16.61—but there are a lot of catches. You can't bring a carry-on, just a personal item, and the seat doesn't recline, or have a seat pocket or a screen. Meaning, Ryanair forces you to confront something far more terrifying than flying: your own thoughts. At least your thoughts are free, because Ryanair charges you for everything else, like checking in at the airport (~$60), snacks, ticket changes, etc. Also, expect little to no customer service. If something goes wrong, you are probably on your own. Their attitude is that by charging for everything the company can reduce the base ticket price to these ultralow levels.

What fascinates me most about the company is how inflammatory Michael O'Leary, Ryanair's CEO, can be. Here are a few fun quotes:

- "Code-sharing, alliances, and connections are all about 'how do we screw the poor customer for more money?'"

- "Air transport is just a glorified bus operation."

- "If drink sales are falling off, we get the pilots to engineer a bit of turbulence. That usually spikes sales."

- "I'm probably just an obnoxious little bollocks. Who cares?"

- "Are we going to say sorry for our lack of customer service? Absolutely not."

- "I should get the Nobel Peace Prize—screw Bono."

You would expect that talking about customers in this way would turn people off; instead, whenever he says something wild, newspapers cover it, and he gets free promotion for the brand. In fact, in 2023, while O'Leary was being interviewed at a conference, climate activists threw a pie in his face. The video of the incident got so much attention that sales on Ryanair jumped 6 percent for the next several days. This is one of the strategies O'Leary used to go from an airline struggling to fly 200,000 people a year to now transporting almost 200 million customers a year. The fact that I am writing this story proves the point; now a lot of people who had never heard of this airline or of O'Leary might get curious.

As you read news headlines you will begin to notice that a lot of CEOs play this game, but just because a few people do, that doesn't mean it works for everyone. If you look across the Fortune 500 you will see that not only have you never heard of most of these massively successful multibillion-dollar companies, but many of their leaders are soft-spoken, and don't try to get attention. So, let's not confuse the examples that show up on social media with what effective leaders are actually like.

The other important factor can be summed up by one business journalist, who after meeting Jack Welch, former CEO of GE, and Andy Grove, former CEO of Intel, in a single week, recounted, "Jeez, are they impressive and stimulating! But am I glad I don't work for them." Intensity is a leadership style some people have, and certain employees thrive in that culture, while others are turned off by it. But being aggressive and intense isn't the only way to behave to be successful; if it's not your style, copying it is a recipe for disaster.

I searched for evidence that being aggressive works in the long run but couldn't find any. If we are going to say something is useful, we also need look for counterexamples. What about all those dominant personalities who didn't succeed, those who failed because their aggression alienated people or, worse, led them to violence or prison.

That's the problem with only looking at successful people; we get confused about what led to their success.

Still, you might be wondering, aren't alphas better negotiators? You might be able to negotiate with someone and "eat their lunch" once, but if you develop a reputation for being a jerk, then the only reason people will interact with you is if they have to. In fact, studies have shown that employees prefer empathetic leaders, and people who are smarter and more generous make for better negotiators.

The 1970s gave us a lot of great things, like disco, ABBA, and Pet Rocks, but some things like asbestosis, indoor smoking, and the "alpha" myth are better left in the past. Let's finally put to rest this inaccurate and damaging obsession with aggressive personalities. Most people don't like to work for them, it doesn't make them more successful, and, as we've seen in the last few years, their behavior could be a liability. It's like putting on a leisure suit from the 1970s—it will make you seem foolish, and if you're not careful when you stand next to a lit candle, you could go up in flames.

So, what type of leadership traits should we look for?

The Right Education

Luckily there is a thriving Ivy League MBA industry, with the smartest researchers and professors in the world getting to the bottom of this. For a modest $150,000–$170,000 and two years out of the workforce with no salary, you could attend Harvard Business School (HBS), Wharton, New York University, the Massachusetts Institute of Technology, Yale, or Stanford. HBS will "educate leaders who make a difference in the world." Meanwhile, Yale will educate people "for business & society." Apparently Yale is better if you don't care about making a difference for the world but want to do something in business. At Stanford you can learn "transformative leadership." Not that anyone knows what that means, but doesn't it sound inspiring?

In all seriousness, I am a huge fan of training and development, but I'm not a fan of wasting time. As Barbara Kellerman, a professor of public leadership at Harvard's Kennedy School of Government, points out, unlike medicine or law there is no general agreement on what defines a leader. There are rigorous standards that doctors, nurses, and pharmacists have to meet to be able to prescribe or handle medication. A doctor can open up a chest cavity and declare with certainty, "That is a heart," but they can't conclude, "That's a heart of a champion." Only Wheaties is qualified to make that call, and until they share their trade secrets with the world, we're all just flying blind here. Amusingly, professionals have to earn a certificate to cut people's hair or serve a hot dog from a cart, but leadership has no minimum level of competence. Think my claim needs a source? Put down this book, watch fifteen minutes of C-SPAN, and then let me know how you feel about our elected leaders' qualifications and skills. So, each of these highly rated MBA programs can and do teach completely different material, to the point that at times they disagree with each other on what makes a great leader.

To make matters worse, it was probably the MBA industry that caused a lot of the confusion around leadership to begin with. Let me explain the ridiculous series of events. Starting in the Second Industrial Revolution (1850–1914), as companies grew so did the need for middle management. These were people who didn't have any specific skills other than managing people. They didn't know how to assemble a car, work an oil rig, or manufacture clothing; they were professional leaders. To most employees, this probably sounded ridiculous—after all, why would you have a leader who didn't have work skills?

So, to legitimize this new class of experts and cash in on the financial opportunity, in 1908 Harvard University started to offer a master's in business administration, aka the MBA. This was supposed to be like a law degree, for leadership, but if you have learned anything reading this book, it's time for a face-palm emoji, because it didn't really work out. Let me correct myself: it worked out very well for Harvard. They made a fortune over the last century, but the education that MBA students receive just doesn't accomplish the promised goal.

Here is what I find frustrating: A master's in accounting teaches people accounting skills, and a master's in social work is supposed to prepare you for a career in social work. According to the research, an MBA doesn't make you a better leader.

The reason might be a fundamental flaw in misunderstanding how people and organizations function. Remember, 1908 was the peak of the Second Industrial Revolution. Society was embracing sciences like chemistry and physics to push our potential and create incredible feats of engineering. New inventions like horseless carriages, lightbulbs, telephones, airplanes, and skyscrapers were revolutionizing society. We were now in command of the natural world; we could even fly. As Duff McDonald, journalist and author of *The Golden Passport,* said, "We took the euphoria of the advancements in the hard sciences and thought we could turn ourselves into machines."

By applying our understanding of science to the social world, Harvard Business School thought it could engineer the perfect leader. Never before had humanity tried to play God for something so lame as a perfect middle management bureaucrat. Their plan was to quantify all the traits of a leader and train them into their students. Just like a car going down an assembly line, by the end of a two-year process, HBS would have a perfect product . . . a leader. After all, this kind of thinking worked well in manufacturing. Since we can standardize the production process, if a part in a machine broke, the company would just replace it with an identical part. A line worker got injured, no problem—just put another person in their place. So, it would make sense that if someone from middle management just went to work for your competitor—no big deal, just put another manager in their place. People were viewed as interchangeable just like the parts of these machines revolutionizing the workplace.

McDonald points out that in hopes of legitimizing HBS as experts in the science of management, in 1926 they hired Elton Mayo, or Dr. Mayo as people called him, to be a professor of industrial research. Mayo was a legend in his own time, and not for the reasons that his last name might suggest. (He did not invent spreadable mayonnaise.)

Instead he became known as the "father of scientific management." What no one realized before he was brought on was that he had faked his credentials. He wasn't a doctor of any kind. He had no PhD, no medical degree, and no real understanding of scientific methods. In fact, the only degree he did have was a bachelor's degree that he earned at about the age of thirty, after flunking out of three medical schools. When he came to the US from his homeland of Australia, the prime minister of Queensland provided him with a letter that wrongly described him as a professor of psychology and physiology. When speaking to the leadership at Harvard, he managed to further convince them he had a medical degree from London. So it shouldn't surprise you that his "research" wasn't that meaningful. If Mayo had devoted his life to the science of lying, he might have actually contributed something of value to humanity.

Instead, Mayo claimed that the interventions he tested on bank employees, factory workers, or day laborers increased their productivity and effectiveness, but that wasn't true since he was either collecting bad data or misunderstanding the results. Instead, what he was seeing would later be called the Hawthorne effect. This is where people change their behavior because someone is paying attention to them. The people he "experimented on" simply worked harder for a while because someone demonstrated interest in their work, or because they were being watched. It wasn't that he had found the science of management; he had just been watching people.

This isn't to say that good research can't be done, but even if the research was more rigorous, the bigger problem is that there is just too much variability from one person to another to reduce the elements of great leadership to a simple formula.

You might be able to engineer almost identical cogs from a machine, but you are starting with the same materials each time you produce a new cog. People have different characteristics, genetics, upbringing, personalities, etc. Expecting everyone to conform to some idea of leadership, and to do it to the same skill level, is unrealistic.

Can we teach people to read or add numbers? Yeah, but anyone who has had to help their kids with homework knows how hard the basics are, and how big a skill gap there is from person to person. Eventually, most people learn to read and add, but remember, those skills are fixed. 1+1 always equals 2. With human beings, 1+1 doesn't add up the same way every time. Two people interacting could be less productive or more productive, depending on their dynamic; they could launch a war or launch a new product or even just ignite romance that dominates office gossip circles for weeks. This complexity can be a real pain or an infuriating challenge, since there are an infinite number of ways people can do something wrong and piss each other off.

MBA programs present the idea that they have done the research and have solved how people function. You take a break from getting actual work experience for two years and they train you in what you are told is a universal set of skills that prepare you to lead. But then, after graduation, a newly minted master of business administration shows up at their new job and interacts with anyone from an auto union in Detroit to a programming team at a tech giant to a private equity firm to a customer service team at Ryanair (just kidding, I don't think they have a customer service team), and they realize that it is a completely different challenge from their case studies and study groups in school.

As Stanford MBA professor Jeffrey Pfeffer and Christina T. Fong of the University of Washington point out in their paper "The End of Business Schools? Less Success than Meets the Eye," "Neither possessing an MBA Degree nor grades earned in courses correlate with career success." They go on to cite study after study. The famed consulting group McKinsey & Company, looking at "people on the job 1, 3, and 7 years, found that at all three points, the people without MBAs were as successful as those with the degree." Meanwhile, the London office of Boston Consulting Group (BCG) found that "non-MBAs were receiving better evaluations, on average, than their peers who had gone to business school," and research by Monitor Consulting "had determined that the people ... hired from high-end business schools were no better at integrative thinking than the undergraduates hired from top-notch liberal arts programs."

Critics will say, "I have an MBA and found it very valuable. Look how much more I earned," or, "Look at the job I got after." I would agree with them: there can be a huge value to getting an MBA. But it just isn't on the skill side of leadership. The potential of higher pay, a more prestigious job after graduation, developing relationships with classmates who will accomplish extraordinary things, and access to impressive alumni networks, to name a few, can have a material impact on a person's career. Possibly the greatest perk is saying, "I went to school in Cambridge" or "just outside of Boston," which is the most humblebrag way of saying you went to Harvard. But let's be clear: there is little to no evidence that MBA training will make you a better leader, and that is the promise that most if not all the top MBA programs make to their applicants.

Let's also acknowledge that MBA programs, especially the most prestigious, are receiving applications from people who are already successful and driven. Let's not confuse the future accomplishments of already impressive people with the education they received in the MBA program. These schools often have a rigorous selection process. They may not be able to pass great leadership skills on to their students, but they are probably able to certify you as a generally impressive person, one that other people should take seriously.

The fact is some people are more skilled at managing than others. Perhaps the key then is not in trying to manufacture the perfect leader by putting them through the MBA assembly line, but in figuring out who has the natural talents needed to be one and help them exercise and deepen those skills.

The Right Type of Leader

In 1921, famed psychologist Carl Jung proposed a theory that people can be broken down into eight different personality types (for example, sensing versus intuition, thinking versus feeling, etc.). At the time psychology didn't use the standards of the scientific method the way it is expected today. There were no peer-reviewed studies, no data-driven analysis, or even any experiments. This was simply a hunch Jung had about people. And who would argue with that? In comparison, there are 98 flavors of Ben & Jerry's ice cream and over 100 kinds of Coca-Cola, but sure, eight ways to categorize a person sounds like enough. Jung saw the flaws of his theories from the beginning. He realized that people didn't neatly fit into one category. He wrote, "Every individual is an exception to the rule."

But much like the true-crime podcasters of our time, a curious mystery novel writer named Isabel Briggs Myers and her mother, a former magazine contributor named Katharine Cook Briggs, thought they could solve the weaknesses in Jung's eight personality types by doubling them to sixteen.

Even though this mother-daughter duo had no formal psychological training, and no clear understanding of science, in 1944 they published *The Briggs Myers Type Indicator Handbook*, later called *The Myers-Briggs*. A guide that answered a question that has vexed people for millennia: Who am I?

Do you want to know who you are? It's easy: take a ninety-two-question survey—for a modest fee, of course—and you will understand:

- *Where you focus your attention:* Extraversion (E) by being sociable or Introversion (I) by focusing inward

- *How you take in information:* Sensing (S) by being more detail-oriented or INtuition (N) by being more abstract

- *How you make decisions:* Thinking (T) through logic or Feeling (F) based on emotions

- *How you deal with the world:* Judging (J) with an ordered system or Perceiving (P) by adapting more

The logic was inescapable. With two types in each category, it means everyone fits into one of sixteen personality types, described by a four-letter combination, and according to the mother-daughter duo, this combo was set from birth. As you read them you may have started seeing where you fit on each of these scales. And if you don't, remember, for a small fee the company that they formed will tell you. You could be ESFJ—the "caregiver" or "consul," described as outgoing, loyal, organized, and tenderhearted—or INFJ, the rarest personality, known as an "advocate" or "idealist." You would be a living contradiction: an easygoing perfectionist, who is both logical and emotional, creative and analytical. The Myers-Briggs Type Indicator (MBTI) played on two innate human qualities: our deep existential need to understand who we are, and our weakness for OSSIs (official-sounding sciency initials). MBTI is so popular that it has been adopted by many government institutions, including the CIA, and a recent count suggests eighty-eight out of the Fortune 100 use it in some way to train, develop, hire, fire, and place employees.

The development of the MBTI was heaven-sent for companies. It had become the gold standard of a massive personality assessment industry that could allow companies to reduce all the confusion of making managerial decisions with an easy-to-solve equation. You need someone to add to a team? Just have people take the MBTI to discover their type, and if it's the right combo, then put them in the role.

When I first heard about these assessments in my twenties, I too was convinced that this was the solution to figuring out what I was going to do with my career. It was like magic: you answer some questions and the "real you" is revealed. I was ready to put on the sorting hat and have it tell me what I always wanted to do with my life. Except, like magic and any great magic show, it was an illusion.

Since consulting companies spend a fortune marketing these types of personality assessments to us, I don't want any confusion about this: they flat out don't work. According to the research, there is no evidence that these kinds of personality tests are even mildly useful. Do you realize how useless something has to be to not even be mildly useful? Even though the result can cause us to feel like we are seen for who we are and what we are capable of. We are unfortunately suffering from a behavioral bias known as the Forer effect.

In 1948, just four years after the release of the MBTI, psychologist Bertram Forer devised a fun experiment. He had thirty-nine students take a comprehensive personality test with the promise that they would get tailored personality assessments based on their answers. A week later the results were presented to the students and rated by them for accuracy. According to their ratings, the assessments were so accurate that on a scale from 0 (very poor) to 5 (excellent), the average accuracy rating was 4.3. What made the results even more impressive is that every person in the class received the same result. There was zero, I repeat zero, personalization. The descriptions included sentences like:

1. You have a great need for other people to like and admire you.

2. You have a tendency to be critical of yourself.

3. You have a great deal of unused capacity which you have not turned to your advantage.

4. While you have some personality weaknesses, you are generally able to compensate for them.

5. At times you have serious doubts as to whether you have made the right decision or done the right thing.

I'm sure you noticed all of us tend to be critical of ourselves, and if we didn't compensate for some of our weaknesses with our strengths, we would be useless. We understand this intuitively from a young age. Kids who aren't considered good-looking may compensate by being funny. Kids who are bad at kickball may gravitate to math. Kids who are good at neither become business-book authors. The results don't describe a specific person; they describe being human. This phenomenon was named after the researcher and became known as the Forer effect (or sometimes the Barnum effect). It is "the tendency to believe that vague predictions or general personality descriptions . . . have specific applications to oneself." So, when MBTI and the like point out a behavior, we think of and remember examples of it. If you tell me I'm a Thinker (T), I will pull memories of the times I thought through problems and ignore the countless times my Feelings (F) were in full control. If you tell me I'm Perceiving (P), which MBTI defines as adaptable, I will remember all those examples of when I adapted to the situation but not all the work I did that was methodically organized, aka Judging (J). You want proof, all I have to do is ask you for examples of emotional decisions, and you will completely forget about the days you were analytical. That's because our brains are great at finding examples and patterns, even if they aren't there.

This is why study after study shows these personality assessments are useless at predicting anything. In fact, one study showed that 50 percent of people who take the test get a different result as few as five weeks later. Even with all the evidence, seventy years later many people are still hiring and firing, staffing people to projects, and promoting based on them.

INFJs, ENFJs, and NFTs all have one thing in common: their value is totally made up. No matter how much easier life would be if we could simply categorize people into neat little buckets, it just doesn't work that way. No one was ever born an INFJ, and they aren't one now, and the reason, put simply, should make sense to anyone: Who we are is too complex to reduce to eight options, sixteen, or any other number. Not only do we change from year to year, but a recent study now shows that our personality changes drastically from one hour to the next. The truth is, we are almost all methodical and adaptive, introverted and extroverted, logical and emotional. A surgeon may be methodical at prepping for surgery, but if they aren't adaptive when an issue comes up, then they can't do their job. An actor can be wildly extroverted onstage but then decompress at home by reading a book. Not only does our personality change based on location, but it also changes based on the time of day, people we are with, our age, and our goals. Are there some trends? Yes, of course, but none of them are strong enough to say if you will be good or bad at leading or having most careers.

The other issue is that this kind of labeling is fundamentally prejudiced. We are disgusted by the idea that a company would deny someone a job based on the color of their skin, but somehow it's okay to deny them a job because a personality assessment that doesn't even work says they are "extroverted." If only they were "introverted," they would have had a place in the company. Unfortunately, any personality assessment you have ever taken or probably ever will take can't quantify whether you can actually do the job required any more than taking the SATs will meaningfully quantify your cholesterol level.

So hopefully now, you can see the train wreck we find ourselves in. We started off thinking there are required skills that make a leader, but every example disproved that. Then we were encouraged to borrow from nature and lead like an alpha, but it turns out the research that inspired that was wrong and the idea is stupid. Then we considered the greatest and most prestigious schools in the world. Unfortunately, not only did they disagree with each other, but their graduates had no improvement over those who never took a single leadership course. Finally, we found no answers in the most popular and pervasive personality assessment. So where does this leave us?

Enter the "authenticity" racket.

Authenticity

I love everything about the modern view of authenticity. This kind of language was originally used to describe genuine artifacts, like an authentic first edition of a rare book or an original painting by a famous painter. But when we talk about people, authenticity suggests that each of us has a pure true self, and when we act consistent with it, we are the person we were meant to be and will accomplish incredible things. We see this over and over again in movies: only by accepting who they truly are can the hero date their love interest, land the dream job, save Gotham, win the ball game, or steal the Declaration of Independence. On the other hand, if we don't align our actions with this genuine version of ourselves, we do not feel right. When our true self is suppressed or ignored, we call that being inauthentic. You have probably seen the trend in companies promoting the notion that we should bring our whole selves or truest selves to the way we lead. This way the workplace can benefit from who we really are.

When I think of authentic leadership, I am reminded of two brothers who had a profound impact both on social issues and on people's lives. If you had met Bob and his brother, growing up in the 1950s and '60s in New York City, you wouldn't have thought much of them. It wasn't until Bob's brother went off to a state school in Buffalo that life began to transform for them. The brothers and their friend Corky started an independent rock concert production company in Buffalo, and in business Bob's brother found himself. He loved to create and provide people with a venue for self-expression. This is where he got to be the truest version of himself, and the money wasn't a bad bonus.

Through the 1970s they put on countless concerts, booking big names like the Rolling Stones, Aerosmith, the Police, and U2. Business was so good that in the late 1970s the brothers and Corky decided to take a big swing. They started an independent art house film production company that would go on to create a series of hit films with real impact. Among them were *The Secret Policeman's Other Ball*, a recording of a benefit concert for Amnesty International that helped raise millions for the international aid organization, and *The Thin Blue Line*, which documented the wrongful conviction of a death row inmate. To their credit, the public attention led to the man's release. By 1993 their company was so successful that Disney purchased it for $80 million, the equivalent of about $170 million today.

Over the next several decades, Bob's brother would go on to earn seven Tony Awards, an Academy Award, and a Golden Globe. He would become the second-most-thanked person in Academy Award acceptance speeches, with only Steven Spielberg getting more, and four spots above God. He earned all of this because he was true to himself and what he loved. I forgot to mention, he also earned a multiyear prison sentence. I neglected to point out that Bob's last name was Weinstein, and his brother was Harvey.

I know this is an upsetting and extreme example, but it reveals the limits of so-called authentic leadership. Notice, no one ever said Harvey was inauthentic. Look back at toxic people who have led organizations and ask yourself if the issue was that they weren't being their truest selves. The problem, if anything, was the opposite—their true selves are dangerous, and they needed restraints on their toxic behavior. Not only is authentic leadership a terrible concept, but as you know and I know, humans aren't that simple. We are way too complex for there to be "one" true self.

Depending on the time of day, how hot it is in the room, how I was raised, when I had my last meal, and a collection of other factors, you will interact with either a lovely version of me or a total jerk. Ask my team: when I get hangry (hunger-induced short-temperedness), I am a different person. It isn't that my authentic self is negatively impacted, as a Snickers ad would have you believe; it's that certain characteristics that I have are coming out more strongly, and my team has the "joy" of interacting with me while I'm being a jerk. The truth is, there is no one true self, because that's not how the brain works. Our brain isn't a single object; it is a collection of systems that specialize in different skills, from seeing and processing language to recognizing faces and processing fear. As they interact with each other, our behavior emerges.

When researchers view brain scans as people are faced with moral challenges, they are able to see different areas of the brain activating and influencing our choices, and depending on a collection of factors, from what culture you were raised in to how people treated you when you entered the building or how hangry you are, different behaviors emerge. It is not that one section is the true us and the other sections are not; all of them are us but sometimes our fear response wins out over our compassion. At times it is good because our fear response saves our lives; other times it's not because we can lash out and hurt people. Much of life is about learning when something is or isn't appropriate. Ultimately if authenticity were stable and permanent behavior like experiencing fear or familiarity, we would be able to pinpoint a specific spot in the brain where it comes from. Despite what all the gurus and fans of the authenticity movement would have you believe, we can't just pick and choose the behaviors we like and say the rest aren't us. Aside from rare cases like brain tumors and drug side effects, *all* our behaviors are ours, and it's our job to manage them—that is the most authentic thing we can say about authenticity.

If authenticity were real, we would be able to measure it. Maybe not through brain scans, but in another way. That's what a group of researchers led by Dr. Erica R. Bailey attempted to do. Imagine you are sitting at a table having a conversation with four to six strangers. After a while, you are asked to rate everyone, including yourself, on how authentic people are. When the results came in, the researchers found an interesting trend. Not only did your rating for your authenticity not match what other people rated you, but their ratings for you didn't match each other. If authenticity was a real characteristic, most people's ratings for you should match each other or at least be close. Instead what we see is that everyone thinks you have a different authentic self.

To make matters more confusing, a research team led by William Hart found that people who self-identify as high on authenticity "seek to appear authentic rather than be authentic." Two hundred forty people were asked to quantify how authentic they viewed themselves and then took a color gazing test. They were told that authentic people will see the colors become more or less intense. Even though the test was fake, and the colors viewed never changed in their intensity, those who self-reported high authenticity either lied or imagined the color intensity change so they would be viewed as more "authentic."

The most that we can say is that people are seen as authentic when they act consistent with the narrative we have of them. It might be easiest to understand by talking about companies. When Pepsi made an ad featuring reality TV star Kendall Jenner that played off the cultural conversation of the Black Lives Matter movement, the internet slammed Pepsi for having no credibility to participate in that conversation. It did not fit the narrative we have of either Pepsi or Kendall Jenner. Meanwhile, when Apple talks about privacy we tend to view it as authentic, because of how many companies they pissed off with their stronger privacy features. Apple's actions seem to fit the narrative.

Unlike huge companies with massive marketing budgets, we have little control over the narratives people have about us. The people in the experiment sitting around the table had different life experiences, biases, and preconceived notions. As a result, the narratives they had for each other didn't match and so their ratings were different.

What we probably mean when we tell leaders and employees to "bring your authentic self to work" is for them to act consistent with their personal narrative. What people tend to pair that with is equity in the way we communicate and express ourselves. For example, if a coworker is in a same-sex relationship, they should be able to talk about their partner to the same degree as heterosexual couples do, and if a person has different political views or comes from a culture where hair is worn differently, they don't want to be penalized or shamed.

Of course, these aren't issues that come up out of a desire to express one's true self, but rather, they come up because people want an equitable right for their narrative to be part of the conversation. Are there exceptions to this? Yes, so don't be annoying and nitpick. If someone is part of an S&M party scene, and another person is part of a wine club, those things aren't equally appropriate to talk about at work, so stop pretending that they are. Also, notice that at no point does this allow for the disgusting behavior that gets excused for people "just being themselves." Certain ways of expressing oneself and behaving are perfectly fine for the workplace, and others aren't. What makes it complicated is that the standards are constantly changing. What was appropriate in the workplace in 1950 is different from 1990, 2020, or what will come next. So, when we talk about authenticity, we also need to talk about what's appropriate for different contexts. Authenticity doesn't exist in a vacuum any more than a leader can exist without followers.

At this point, you may be thinking, well, if nothing works—from alpha leadership, MBAs, personality assessments, and even authenticity—then why bother trying to be a better leader? If you are thoroughly bummed out, then I think we have accomplished the goal of this chapter. Your illusions have been shattered—about work, leadership, and the very nature of the self. Don't worry, the existential crisis means it's working. Now that we have cleared out many of the biggest misconceptions, we can get to the fun part: discovering what matters when it comes to leadership and how you can apply it to unlock team intelligence.

Ideas in Action

- Much of what we have been taught about leadership isn't true.

- Being an aggressive alpha is more of a liability than a benefit. People don't want to work for them or negotiate with them and mimicking them leads to problems.

- We hear about certain CEOs because the media likes to cover sensational behavior. Don't confuse what gets attention for what actually works.

- Although MBA programs promise to create leaders, the research shows that graduates don't perform better as leaders. There are valuable things a person can get from an MBA, but being a better leader isn't one of them.

- Trying to train a leader outside of a work environment may be a pointless task.

- Using personality assessment tests also doesn't work since the results aren't meaningful, and more importantly, they can't predict people's future performance.

- The trend of authentic leadership falls flat since the research shows there is no authentic self. At best, authenticity is acting consistent with the narrative others have for you.

Chapter 2
Why Should Anyone Follow You?

Chances are this chapter will fill you with clarity, disappointment, and hope. We will finally discuss what makes a leader. But let me ask one important question: Why on earth would you want to be a leader?

When interviewing executives and researchers for this book, one of the most consistent findings was that leading people is not for everyone. If you work at a creative agency, there is a big difference between coming up with award-winning advertisements and running the agency. One is a creative role, and the other is management and logistics. If you dreamed of being a creative or an artist, then spending 90 percent of your week dealing with accounting and staffing problems probably isn't appealing. We have been sold on the idea that everyone should want to be promoted to a leadership role, without asking if it's the type of work we would enjoy or care about.

So why do we do this to ourselves? Part of the problem is that starting salaries might not be enough to support ourselves or our families. The bigger reason is probably that humans are obsessed with status. The scientific argument is that we are wired so that everything we do is in hopes of gaining status because with it comes better mating choices and better chances for survival. Few things signal more status than having a large audience, devoted followers, and the automatic influence and power that come with a fancy title or top spot on the organizational chart. You might reply, "Jon, I don't care about status." To that I would say you are probably lying, because every culture in the world is obsessed with it.

In 1948, after returning from the Micronesian island of Pohnpei (at the time called Ponape), anthropologist William R. Bascom reported his discovery of one of my favorite cultural traditions. On Pohnpei, much of a man's status depended on what he contributed to the local chief's feasts. But that's not the interesting part. Even though Pohnpei is incredibly fertile and has lots of local natural food sources (seafood, coconuts, breadfruit, etc.), the only food anyone really cares about is yams. In this case, it's not the number of yams—it's sheer size of a man's yam. That's not a euphemism.

According to Bascom, at the local chief's feasts, "Everyone present examines and compares the yams as they are brought into the feast house, and praises the largest yam for its size and quality. They go up to the man who, in their opinion, brought the best yam to tell him that he is 'Number One.' The commoners praise him for his skill and ability as a farmer; the chief praises him for his generosity."

These yams are huge and can reach ten feet long and three feet in diameter. Locally, they are measured by the number of men it takes to carry them, with one report of a yam reaching 100 kilograms (220 pounds).

One reason for such fierce competition is that the men who consistently contribute large yams are promoted with an official district title, once one opens up. It is how you move up in society. Just imagine the drama: If a man were to insult another person's yams, it would be an insult to his very status, so the locals never display their biggest and best. This way, if they are challenged, they can come back the next year and show how skilled they are by presenting even bigger prizes. Bascom points out in his report that "if the challenger has not brought larger yams himself, he is publicly shamed." Yes, you read that right. Public shaming is the result of a failed yam-off.

With a person's position in society at stake, yams must be grown in secret, often in overgrown areas of a farm so no one can see them. How someone grows their yams is considered a trade secret. Also, "it is impolite to look at another man's yams, and anyone caught doing so will feel the shame of gossip and ridicule."

At first this example might seem strange—like a confusing waste of time—but if we're being honest, many of us can admit that if we lived in this society, we might become equally *obsessed* with yam growing. Or having a bigger swimming pool than the neighbors or a fancier car—you name it. We can't escape the status game, from designer shoes and hype-brand clothing to fancy cars and technology to how low your license plate number is. In Dubai, someone bought the license plate P7 for $15 million, because of the status of a low number. Even saying we don't care about status is in itself a status identifier.

So, before you step up for that next promotion to a leadership role, ask yourself if you want it because you really want to win this season's yam-off or because you actually care about leading people. Despite what you might have been told, there are other ways to excel at work and to develop status without having to lead large organizations. Instead of growing the number of people who report to you, you can, for instance, focus on developing mastery in your craft or becoming a person others turn to for book recommendations. That said, many people would enjoy the work of leading and are looking to develop these skills further, in which case: go for it. But what, exactly, are you going for?

What Makes a Leader

The answer may seem annoyingly simple, but it is as difficult to assemble as an Ikea bookcase. One complication is that we use the term *leader* in a variety of ways—from political leader and business leader to thought leader or dance leader, and we have different relationships with each of them.

Let's start with an analogy and a question: What makes someone a parent?

This isn't a trick question. The answer is: a child. So, what makes someone a leader? All they need is someone who follows them. It sounds annoyingly simple, but now for the complicated part.

There is a big gap between someone having children to parent and someone being a great parent you admire. There is also a gap between someone having followers to lead and someone being a great leader you actually want to follow even if your job doesn't depend on it. One can stunt your social and emotional development, threaten your access to the vital resources you need to survive, and leave you with emotional trauma that you work through in therapy for the rest of your life. The other is a parent.

So, what fills that gap? What makes you want to follow someone? What makes someone want to follow you?

You might want to give an answer like, they were bigger than life or charismatic, or maybe it is about the incredible impact they had. When I ask for examples, people often mention the same names: Martin Luther King Jr., Mahatma Gandhi, Abraham Lincoln, and of course, a petite Albanian woman named Anjezë Gonxhe Bojaxhiu.

Anjezë (or as we would say, Agnes) was born in 1910, in what is now North Macedonia. At the age of twelve she felt a strong call to God, an intense need to "spread the love of Christ." So, six years later she joined a mission that would go to Calcutta (today Kolkata), in the Bengal region of India. After taking her vows, she chose to be named after Thérèse de Lisieux, the patron saint of missionaries, and for seventeen years (1931–48) Teresa taught in Calcutta at St. Mary's High School.

Seeing the intense poverty, hunger, disease, and suffering outside the school's walls was devastating for Teresa. As if things weren't bad enough, during her time there, World War II led to the Bengal famine of 1943, where an estimated three million people in the region died. It was a humanitarian crisis, and she felt her place was with the people, having a direct impact. So she asked her superiors to let her operate independently and help those who needed her most.

There she was, a five-foot-tall nun standing in the streets of Calcutta, organizing the poorest of the poor into an open-air school for the children in the slums. What made her shine wasn't the traditional trappings of title or status; instead she had shown traits that seemed foreign to most—namely, unrelenting effort and unreasonable selflessness. And thanks to these traits people would take notice and then volunteer to join her efforts. As the story of the legendary nun spread, so did the donations. In a short time, Teresa was able to expand her operations, raising money for those who needed medical care, and building a home for the dying and destitute.

In the following years, her work touched countless people's lives, thanks to her incredible leadership. A 1969 BBC documentary about her, titled *Something Beautiful for God*, was released, and a book by the same name came two years later. Soon after, she became a global phenomenon.

Between then and her death in 1997 she would go on to not only raise hundreds of millions of dollars for her cause, and expand her missionary work to over one hundred countries, but she would also be awarded the Nobel Peace Prize. World leaders, celebrities, and business titans flocked to meet this selfless and unrelenting holy woman and support her work of giving life and dignity to all those who were forgotten and overlooked. Nine years after her death, the Vatican canonized her sainthood, Teresa having in their eyes performed two miracles. On the hundredth anniversary of her birth, the Indian government issued a five-rupee coin in her honor, the same amount of money she had when she came to India. President Pratibha Patil of India said that Mother Teresa "became a symbol of hope to many—namely, the aged, the destitute, the unemployed, the diseased, the terminally ill, and those abandoned by their families."

So, what was it that caused people to follow the woman who became known as Mother Teresa? In the early days, she had neither money, fame, or status and she wasn't the most charming person. To this day, her group, Missionaries of Charity, with thousands of nuns and priests, still operates 760 homes in 139 countries. By any standard, she was considered a global leader, and yet she didn't have any of the characteristics that we tend to think of when we talk about leadership. I would argue that the answer lies in a quirk of human behavior, one that you have experienced hundreds of times before.

To understand Mother Teresa's success I'm going to take you on quick detour back to being a teenager. I want you to imagine yourself in high school and it is Friday afternoon at about 1. p.m. How do you feel? Even though you are sitting in school, you are excited for the weekend. Maybe you're going to a party or you can't wait to check on your yams. Now think about how you felt Sunday at 6 p.m. Even though you are free, you are upset because the future is school or work—this is why we get the "Sunday scaries." Our experience of life is based on the future we think we have, and so we follow someone like Mother Teresa because of how they make us feel. Specifically, we follow someone who makes us feel that there will be a new or better future than the one we think we have now.

When people interacted with Mother Teresa, they felt something new was possible. This woman would personally clean the unhoused so that they could have dignity. Notice, I didn't say that they give us a logically reasoned argument. That doesn't really work. Mother Teresa didn't call a meeting to give a PowerPoint presentation listing all the facts about why we should help, because that doesn't get us to *feel* anything, other than the feeling that some meetings should just be an email.

We follow someone because we feel that something new is possible. If you can help people feel that they will earn more, grow bigger yams, have more career success, raise better children, defeat their nemesis, or at least make their ex envious, they will follow you.

And when a little unrelenting and selfless five-foot-tall nun in Calcutta showed the world that we can love the most forgotten people and give them dignity, her following grew because they felt there was a new future for humanity . . . if only we just followed her.

Notice that I also didn't say a leader needs to accomplish anything. Producing results versus making people *feel* that the result will be produced are two completely different things. Leaders who gain followers just have to make us *feel* like we will have a better future. If we only measured good leadership through the results it produced, we probably would reduce the pay of many CEOs. Then again, if we judged CEOs exclusively by how they make their workers feel, we would still probably dock many of their salaries.

Similarly, if we evaluated the results that Saint Teresa of Calcutta produced, we probably wouldn't follow her either. After her passing, a few key pieces of information came to light in credible books, documentaries, and newspaper articles.

Do you remember the estimated hundreds of millions of dollars—if not more—that people donated, making her charity one of the best funded in the world? It is well documented that little of the money went to caring for the poor and sick. Even though the public image of Teresa was tied to Calcutta as the savior of the poor, most of the money raised went to missionary work to convert people to Catholicism.

Even with countless millions in the bank, the few poor and sick whom they did care for were given virtually no medical care. Those with infectious diseases were not isolated, causing the disease to spread. When syringes were used, they were washed in water (not sterilized).

Non-Catholic patients, at the end of their lives, would be secretly tricked into being baptized without consent. Staff would come with a wet cloth pretending to clean their heads and would perform the ritual. You know how some parents promised their kids ice cream on a Sunday morning, only to drag them to church? Mother Teresa scaled that racket like a tech VC.

She believed that "pain, sorrow, suffering are but the kiss of Jesus—a sign that you have come so close to Him that He can kiss you." And so even with the budget to eliminate pain, and the public persona of someone who cared for those no other would care for, she would let people suffer in terrible pain, so they might be closer to God. Whether or not she was a great leader is not for me to judge. I take that back: I am absolutely here judging her. Otherwise I wouldn't have written about her, but the answer depends on your values.

I can imagine that this so-called saint believed that her most important role in the world was to bring Jesus to the masses, and so justified violation after violation of trust. You may even agree with her, but that's not the point.

I chose this story because it perfectly illustrates the gap between our *perception* of a leader and the actual person. We have been told for generations that leaders are people with lists of noble traits, and if you go to a good training program you will come out with those skills, and people will follow you.

Her story emphasizes two things. The first is that people don't follow those noble traits. Instead we are so driven by emotion that we will follow someone we feel will give us a new future, even if they don't deliver it. It also shows us how terrible we are distinguishing emotional responses from objective results. This paradox explains the existence of cult leaders, unethical politicians, business charlatans, and all sorts of people who convince us to follow them into the future.

People describe leadership as some noble pursuit, but when we take out all the morality, and stories we have told ourselves, we get to the central question any aspiring leader should be asking: "If what defines a leader is having followers, and we follow because we feel there is a new future, do I have the skills I need to have people follow me and feel they have a new future?" The answer may surprise you: it is a very strong MAYBE!

I think I'm doing a terrible job leading right now, since you might not be convinced you have a new future if you keep reading, so let me try again.

The answer is a resounding YES! But we need to understand what causes someone to feel that they have a new future, because if we can learn that, we can lead. If you look at the most famous and most effective leaders, they don't share any consistent skills or behaviors. Every leader seems to have a different style, so what do we focus on?

The Math of Leadership

To understand the answer, let's take another quick trip back in time. In the spring of 1913, Anna and Lajos Erdős were working as math teachers in Budapest, Hungary. They were expecting their third child, and as the due date approached, both of their daughters (three and five years old) began to get sick. On the day Anna gave birth to their son, Paul, tragedy hit, and both of their girls died of scarlet fever. The unbelievable pain and trauma of losing them made Anna protective of Paul. Paranoid that she would lose him too, for the first ten years of his life she wouldn't let him out of the house, go to school, or play with other children. As if the family hadn't suffered enough hardship, when Paul was about one and a half his father was captured and put in a Soviet prisoner-of-war camp for six years.

So, while his mother was out teaching math, Paul sat alone at home with no one to keep him company but his parents' collection of math books. It was from these books that Paul was able to teach himself to read. He would later say that "numbers became my best friends."

In 1934, at the age of twenty-one, Paul earned his PhD in mathematics from the University of Budapest. Being Jewish and seeing the rise of antisemitism and World War II looming, he realized he had to leave Europe. He was able to secure a position at Princeton, but it meant that he left his family behind. Back in Europe, when the Nazis arrived in Budapest they killed his father, along with four out of five of his mother's siblings.

He was now alone in the US, and the only real living connection he had in the world, his mother, was stuck in Nazi-controlled Hungary. Paul was incredibly lonely, and because of his insanely overprotective mother, he never developed normal social skills. He had no traditional friendships, and he didn't date. All he had was work.

You would expect that this level of trauma, loneliness, and isolation would break a person. But rather than sit in depression, Paul did the one thing he knew how to do . . . math.

The only people he had any contact with were his fellow mathematicians, so he turned problem-solving into a joyous community experience. He started connecting with people working on interesting math problems, and he would find a way to go meet them. Paul would quite literally show up at their door and say what became his catchphrase: "My brain is open." Then the two would create new and exciting work together.

Through these adventures Paul would travel across twenty-five different countries, meeting absolute strangers and solving math problems with them. He eventually gave up almost all of his possessions and even his home. Now, as I describe Paul's adventures, you may be thinking, What an extraordinary person. He was able to turn tragedy into an opportunity to connect and make an impact. Yes, that is true, but in almost every other aspect, his visits were a nightmare none of us would want to experience.

Remember, Paul had no social skills; he grew up alone with only math as a companion. He was also unhoused, so everywhere he went he was completely dependent on the people who hosted him. When I say completely dependent, I mean that he had no idea how to cook, or even boil water to make a hot drink, and he couldn't change his clothing. Apparently he also suffered from an uncomfortable skin condition that meant that he could only wear silk clothing, but don't think for a moment that he knew how to wash his clothes, which meant that the host had to carefully do Paul's laundry for him.

As if that wasn't already the premise for an Oscar-winning film starring Joaquin Phoenix, Paul had another eccentric habit: he also wouldn't sleep. According to the biography of his life, he spent 20–22 hours a day doing math. He would bang pots and pans in the kitchen in the middle of the night just to wake you up to do more work. This man was clearly the guest from hell! If he were alive today, he would probably be the only man to ever have a subzero guest rating on Airbnb. And yet people flocked for the chance to host him. This should fill you with confidence about your potential. Paul had none of the traits we associate with leadership. In fact, he had many qualities that actively pushed people away, and yet people followed.

You may be asking, What was so special about working with Paul Erdős? And here we begin to get a hint at what caused people to follow him. Those who collaborated with him described it as a religious experience. He somehow was able to understand how people thought and to lean on those strengths to bring out their best. It wasn't that he had lists of skills from an MBA, but rather it was his ability to collaborate that caused people to feel there was a new future. When people worked with Paul, they were on a journey to find the great mathematical truths of the universe. His biographer described him at a math conference, sitting in his hotel room working with ten to twelve mathematicians spread across any open spot from the beds to the floor. Each was working on a separate problem, and Paul would continuously jump between them, simultaneously working to find solutions with everyone. These aren't simple high school equations; these are many of the most complex problems around, and everyone who collaborated with him became smarter in the process.

Paul was so incredible at working with others that he published and collaborated on more academic papers than anyone in the history of mathematics. Paul died at the age of eighty-three, but for his eightieth birthday, his collaborators assembled to celebrate the man who had guided them. The lonely, socially awkward, isolated boy grew up to be loved and followed by so many that to this day at math conferences, people will identify themselves by their "Erdős number." This number represents how close you are to having worked with Paul. An Erdős number of 1 means you and Paul published a paper together, 2 means you published with someone who worked with Paul, and so on. When you count ring after ring, you realize that there are about 200,000 people with Erdős numbers. Each of them was touched in some way by Paul's work and leadership. If you were curious, I am a 4 both in terms of my Erdős number and my looks.

So why put up with Paul? Why follow him? Why do his laundry and be woken up in the middle of the night by a pots and pans drum solo? His *New York Times* obituary said: "His colleagues took care of him, lending him money, feeding him, buying him clothes, and even doing his taxes." Paul lacked almost all the essential leadership characteristics that we are told we must have (being organized, strategic, flexible, effective at time management, etc.), but what he did have were two skills that were so disproportionately strong that others were willing to overlook his weaknesses for the chance to experience magic: he loved math to the point that nothing else mattered and he knew how to get the best from others. That combination of super skills was his gift.

As I was researching these ideas, I realized that anyone who has all of these "essential" leadership traits doesn't stand out. If you are good at everything, you aren't great at anything. But if you are amazing at one or two things, it can inspire people to follow you. Elon Musk, the richest person in the world at the time I'm writing this sentence, isn't known for being empathetic or flexible; instead he has one or two skills that are so disproportionately strong that when he speaks you might feel the possibility of a new future. Musk thinks at scale and acts faster than anyone in our culture, so when he says he is going to Mars, people feel that he can do it and say, "I will follow." It might be by buying stock from one of his companies, clicking follow on X, or going to work for him.

This is why the world's worst house guest could travel anywhere, all the while inspiring and leading the math world to new discoveries. Paul's obituary went on to explain that for those who cared for him, "In return, he showered them with ideas and challenges—with problems to be solved and brilliant ways of attacking them." His friend and collaborator Joel Spencer said, "He was a Saint. . . . He gave faith to those of us who are doing mathematics . . . that we were trying to find Truth, a truth that transcends the physical universe."

Paul's super skills were so extraordinary that when you worked with him, no matter how difficult it was, he would make you feel like you had a new future. That's what leadership is about . . .

Each leader may have completely different super skills and still be able to achieve greatness. Famed founder Bill Gates is known for his structured thinking and curiosity. These super skills led him to cofound Microsoft, one of the most valuable companies in the world, and the Bill & Melinda Gates Foundation, commonly viewed as a shining example of philanthropic efforts. Meanwhile, Wangari Muta Maathai was known for her resoluteness and incorruptibility, which fueled her to found the Green Belt movement. Her organization is one of the most effective deforestation prevention programs in the world and fought for democracy in Kenya opposing Daniel arap Moi's regime, which is commonly viewed as dictatorial. For her efforts she received the 2004 Nobel Prize, making her the first African woman in history to earn the award. These are examples of global leaders, but the same principle holds for being a leader of a community, a team, or a family. If you can identify and cultivate your special skills, you too can become a leader. And more crucially, like Erdős you might never have to do laundry again.

I should also point out that just because followers are attracted to the future that a leader promises, it doesn't guarantee they will enjoy the journey. One of Elon Musk's employees described the trade-offs in working with him: "I had the choice between being burnt out and being bored, and I decided I want to be burnt out because I believed in the mission."

When we begin to realize how different each leader's super skills are from each other, it explains why trying to mimic a successful leader or applying their advice is often useless. It may work for their super skills but just doesn't match what you would be good at.

Are there many skills that would be helpful and potentially make us even more effective? Absolutely. Could you improve your skills? Without a doubt, and over a career you will hopefully work on useful skills and experience the joy of growth and development. But it's important to separate what is essential from what is nice to have. When it comes to leadership in the corporate world, nothing is essential, and trying to achieve mastery or even competence in something we are never going to be exceptional at is probably a waste of time that would stunt your leadership potential. Instead, much like any leader, you have some skills that are so disproportionately strong that when you use them, you shine.

Finding My Super Skills

Now, you may be asking, What are *my* super skills?

To that I say, I'm sorry, but I don't know you. Unless I do know you, in which case thank you for following through on saying that you would buy a copy of my book. Even so, this is a book, not a conversation. Unless you live in the world of Harry Potter, you can't expect an answer to that question from a book, but I do have a really simple solution to this: call up your friends and coworkers and ask them:

"What do you think are my strongest skills? Just to be clear, I don't mean that I make amazing PowerPoint decks, or I am a great accountant. Those are the results of the skill. For example, someone who is empathetic can imagine how other people would hear an idea and then is able to make great PowerPoint decks. Someone who is good at seeing the flaws in a system might be an incredible accountant because they spot all the loopholes. What do you think are my skills?"

You may notice that the same skills will keep showing up, and that will give you a hint of what yours might be. But to provide a fair warning, the idea of super skills isn't set in stone. A super skill is more like a really strong tendency. It also isn't a skill like raising money. You might be amazing at raising money because your skill is that you are a fantastic storyteller, and that translates well to pitching. But you will notice great storytelling can help in being a CEO or a marketer or a parent in the way you share ideas. The goal of this exercise isn't in pigeonholing you into a role, but rather in giving you permission to flex your strongest muscles when appropriate to accomplish whatever you want to. The Hulk might smash. But he could also apply his super strength to a variety of crafts like welding, dog walking, piano moving, or chiropracting.

Just because you have a skill doesn't mean you can use it in every situation. A misapplied skill is a liability. If you are really great at motivating people by cheering them, your cheerleading skills can lead to your team feeling very supported, having high levels of psychological safety, and wanting to contribute their best work, but it might not be helpful at a funeral.

My ability to create belonging is really enjoyable in almost every group, but it is terrible if I'm surrounded by psychopaths. I would probably like them all and they would take advantage of me. Does it mean that all we need are super skills? No, of course not. There are many additional skills, habits, and abilities we develop and refine over a lifetime, and they are incredibly useful. I used to be a terrible public speaker. In my early teens, I would cry any time I would get in front of a crowd. I cannot express how embarrassing that was; I still cringe thinking about it. Now I speak professionally, and I am incredibly proud to say that I put in a lot of effort and now my reviews are absolutely stellar. Growth and improvement are critical to a long career. The point of discussing super skills is to understand that those skills are likely the reason people will follow you, and to take the pressure off of trying to be perfectly well-rounded with a set of skills that aren't essential. In the next chapter, we will explore how to improve and what to focus on, but first we should understand how to use our super skills.

Think about it like this, when you watch any heist film the team is made up of people with different skills. The safecracker doesn't try to be a master of disguise or a pickpocket. Working by themselves, each of them can only accomplish some small-time thefts (if that), but as a team, they can dream bigger. They always seem to be after that one final score, the one that will let them retire.

What we used to believe is that there are certain skills that make a leader different than the rest of us. Unfortunately, Hollywood usually puts an attractive, charming, or charismatic star in the role, but now we know better. Hopefully I've convinced you that any type of person can be a leader, even the not hot ones (believe me, I'm living proof!). Any one of the team members could be the leader, and for them to lead, all they need is for people to feel there will be a new future, and the team will follow them.

You may be thinking, Okay, I get it, Jon, I need to lean into my super skills when appropriate, but there is a big difference between a leader that can put a crew together for a heist and one that gets away. I want to lead a team that is effective. The kind of team that is more than the sum of its parts, one that has high team intelligence. How do I develop myself to be that leader?

The solution is twofold. First, focus on growth. We all have areas where improving them will make us and our teams more effective. It can range from the way we connect with employees/customers and the way we give feedback to how we present or share our vision. It is important to realize that real growth requires effort and takes time. If you know there are certain skills that if improved would make a big difference, the next chapter is all about that. I searched for the most important factors you can put in place and found a surprising area that most of us should start with. That's what is next.

Second, focus on your team. To be an effective leader is about getting the team to operate at its best. It is about maximizing team intelligence. Ideally, you surround yourself with people who have the skills you lack. With the right dynamics, you can pull off the heist and make it out safe. We will explore this in depth in Part II.

One final thing: You do know that heist thing is just an analogy, right?

Ideas in Action

- Ask yourself, do you want the challenge of leading, or is this just for status?

- Only one thing consistently defines a leader: followers.

- We follow someone when we *feel* that they will give us a new and better future. Whether the leader delivers results is something else entirely.

- Leaders have one or two super skills that are inordinately strong, which explains why no two leaders are alike (and why the search for the "essential traits of leadership" is a mirage).

- Look to your team to make up for skills you may lack.

Chapter 3

Growing Your Skills

Any serious basketball fan knows the name Draymond Green. He is a superstar player for the Golden State Warriors with four championship rings (that's as many as LeBron James). He is a four-time NBA All-Star and a two-time Olympic gold medalist, and is considered one of the best defensive players in the league. Are there things that he can do to improve? Absolutely, but I wouldn't know because even with all the sports stories I share, I have never watched a game. What I do understand is that at the intensity that professionals like Draymond train and work on their skills, it is hard to imagine there will be massive gains, considering they are already pushing the limits of the human body. So how do you take an exceptional player like Draymond and make him better? Where do you focus when someone has already honed their skills to the apex of excellence?

Let's go back to the parenting analogy I brought up in the last chapter. When someone has their first child, everyone gives them every piece of unwanted advice you can imagine. They are fed lists of must-do activities for fear that their child will fail at life. Parents need to read with their children every day, maintain an ideal sleep schedule, set limits, and make sure their children eat vegetables—the requirements of parental perfection never end. I'm sure the research shows every one of these things is important, but if we are honest, all these good things won't make up for harmful parenting behaviors. Verbally abusing a child isn't forgotten by reading them a few books, and the trauma of neglect isn't canceled out by making sure they eat more vegetables. When it comes to our relationships, especially when there is an uneven power dynamic, the impact of our negative behavior tends to be much worse than the good done by our positive behavior.

This brings us back to how we improve Green's game. The biggest gain isn't going to be refining his ability to steal the ball. In 2017 he led the league in that feat. Instead, his biggest improvements are likely to come by focusing on the other side of the equation: what he does that has a negative impact on the team. Draymond has a reputation for getting in trouble. Some sports critics have even said, "His signature move is the groin kick," a cool reputation in WWE wrestling but not so much appreciated in the NBA. He has punched players, stomped on them, and committed tons of hard fouls. At 6'6" and 230 pounds, he is a wall of muscle—taller and bigger than Mike Tyson or Muhammad Ali at their peak. It doesn't matter who you are—a hit from him is going to hurt. During the 2023–24 season, after hitting a player in the face, the NBA gave him an indefinite suspension for his "repeated history of unsportsmanlike acts." And here we have our answer. If you want the biggest improvement to Draymond's game, it's not in refining what he is already masterful at. You might get a small boost, and he is probably already working on that. The big difference is making sure he stops getting kicked out of the game for playing dirty. Not to state the obvious, but being the best at something is useless if you aren't even allowed to do that thing.

So, if you want to win more, the coach has to find a way to get him to stop breaking the rules of the NBA and the social contract we all share (a contract that, last time I checked, does not look kindly at groin kicks). In perhaps one of the most outrageous breaches of trust, Green punched his own teammate during practice. The Warriors had just won their fourth championship. Many believe that this incident and Green's outrageous behavior derailed the team's chemistry, causing them to underperform the following year.

In business, the same issues come up, although hopefully without the threat of violence. With good intentions, we try to help leaders improve their skills—skills like time management, communication, and giving feedback—but these are skills most leaders are already doing fairly well. The opportunity is only for small gains over time. The real opportunity—the fastest way to improvement—is to focus on softening the poor habits that harm team success.

Do you want proof? Think back to any time your boss or a coworker made you feel small, stupid, or embarrassed. Maybe they yelled at you or shamed you in front of others. Maybe it didn't happen to you directly, but you saw it happen to someone else. Think about how uncomfortable you felt when you saw someone being yelled at or humiliated.

No one wants to work for someone who belittles, humiliates, verbally abuses, or threatens them. It signals that we are no longer safe, and that we are not part of the group. When leaders breach the social contract, then we aren't motivated to engage, and may be scared too. Darth Vader from *Star Wars* had a lot of flaws. He betrayed his friends and massacred millions. But let's not forget, he was also a terrible boss. When one of his Imperial Officers failed him, he would immediately choke them to death. No feedback, not even a performance improvement plan, just straight to murder. How do you think employee morale was on the giant space base he oversaw, known as the Death Star? This kind of work culture can lead to catastrophic failure, as I'll explain in a bit.

When researchers at Google looked at the greatest predictor of team success, it wasn't time socializing outside the office, shared hobbies, or educational backgrounds; it was psychological safety. The simplest way to describe it: team members feel safe sharing an idea that goes against the group without the fear of being punished, or pushed out. Psychological safety is an essential element that preserves the social contract.

The example almost every book uses to demonstrate poor psychological safety is the tragedy of the space shuttle *Challenger*, when on January 28, 1986, due to a faulty seal, the shuttle disintegrated during takeoff. All hands were lost. The issue was a known problem that engineers were too uncomfortable to keep bringing up. In this case, it wasn't verbal or physical abuse that blocked them, but rather a culture of ignoring and downplaying problems. Or consider this other tragedy of space exploration.

In the not-so-cold war for space dominance, a plan was developed to build a permanent base in space. Ships would be able to land, drop off personnel and supplies, and then return or go on nearby missions. Unfortunately, the design and construction teams were absolutely terrified of the project manager. When the designs for the base were being developed, the engineering team built it with a fatal flaw, a thermal exhaust port that if ignited would cause a chain reaction and blow up the entire base. Let's be clear about this: the flaw is so flagrant that it could only happen if people were scared to speak up. Which is why on May 25, 1977, a group of rebels, under the orders of Princess Leia Organa, were able to attack the imperial base known as the Death Star. Spoiler alert: her twin brother, Luke Skywalker, fired two proton torpedoes into the thermal vent, leading to the destruction of the base and the death of an estimated two million people. You might be wondering who was in charge of the base. It was none other than everyone's least favorite boss, and most terrifying man in the empire, Darth Vader. Unless you have been living under a rock, I haven't spoiled the plot of *Star Wars*. The only thing more ridiculous than this example is how perfectly it demonstrates the importance of psychological safety.

I'm not trying to suggest that any of us are abusive to our employees, although some people are. A 2020 study by the International Labour Organization found that 26 percent of workers worldwide have experienced workplace violence or harassment in the past year. Up from 22 percent in 2010. It won't surprise you that women were more likely to be the victims than men. A Gallup survey from 2022 found that 23 percent of workers experience violence or harassment at work. Sure, being yelled at sucks, but what's worse is that 38 percent of women and 14 percent of men have reported experiencing sexual harassment at work.

Obviously, these are upsetting statistics, and you may even be wondering how these extreme examples relate to your workplace. Let's face it: we can all be jerks at times, all humans are. We get annoyed, short-tempered, and say things that we regret. The hopeful message I'd like you to hear is that we can make small improvements and modest adjustments in our negative behaviors that produce a large and lasting impact.

Personally, I am not prone to yelling or even being upset at my employees. But about fifteen years ago, I did notice I would respond in a way I didn't like. Something would happen, a project would go wrong, a person would screw up, and then I would ask questions. It would look like I was trying to find an answer, but really the questions would make them feel bad and incompetent. Frankly, it was a nasty behavior. In comparison to Darth Vader, my breach of the social contract was small, but it wasn't healthy, and I didn't like myself after I did it.

What I realized, and what other experts will tell you, is that it doesn't help to say, "I will never do it again," because the moment we get upset, it's too late. We are like the Incredible Hulk on a rampage—even though we know, even as we're rampaging, that our methods are having a harmful effect. You might think that the most immediate solution is to head out on a vision quest, light some sage to clear the bad vibes, or visit your favorite therapist. No doubt these tactics might be helpful, but if it's immediate and proven methods you seek, then you need to look outward, not inward. You need to build an automatic system that doesn't let these tendencies wreak havoc. I can't tell you what to do about anger management or other terrible habits because I'm not with you to understand the problem you are dealing with, but I will share what I found helpful.

Build a Better System

In 1994, US Air Force test and fighter pilot Terry Virts was flying a training mission in South Korea. The objective was to practice using a special targeting system, while at the same time flying his F-16. As if it's not hard enough to fly one of the most advanced jets in the world during ideal conditions, Terry had to do it at night and at low altitude, meaning close to the ground, while simultaneously controlling a targeting system. It's like playing basketball and football at the same time. If you lose focus for just a second while trying to shoot a layup, a guy the size of a mountain will tackle and crush you.

Terry was flying at hundreds of miles an hour over his objective, and as he switched his focus to the targeting system, he took his attention away from the ground. Without his realizing it, a literal mountain had appeared in front of him, but he was too focused on the targeting system to notice he was about to crash and die.

This is one of the terrible and great things about the human brain. We can create habits, good or bad, that become so automatic, that even when we are hurtling toward a mountain, we don't notice or can't stop ourselves. I'm sure you notice that once we are stuck in a habit, it's not just as simple as stopping. It's unfair to expect ourselves to not fall into our routines. If I want to eat healthy and someone keeps leaving desserts out on my kitchen counter, I'm eventually going to eat the desserts. More willpower can only get us so far when trying to change behavior.

If you were to guess the leading cause of death for F-16 pilots, you would imagine enemy fire, technical issues, or heat-seeking missiles, but it is something far more tragic. According to the US Air Force, flying into the ground makes up 26 percent of aircraft losses and an incredible 75 percent of all F-16 pilot deaths.

Part of the reason is that it is really hard to pay attention to everything when the stakes are so high. Another reason is something called G-LoC, or Gravity-induced Loss of Consciousness. When a pilot turns at high speed, the intense forces on their body cause the blood to move away from their brains and to their arms and legs. They get suddenly lightheaded and can lose consciousness, causing them to fly into the ground.

Eventually, after so many pilot deaths, engineers were able to develop Auto G-Cas, or Ground Collision Avoidance System. With Auto G-Cas installed on a plane, their flight controls are tied into the navigation system. If the plane sensors notice that you are getting dangerously close to the ground, Auto G-Cas automatically kicks in and pulls up.

Thanks to this technology, many lives have been saved and hundreds of millions of dollars in fighter jets are still in use. It is the reason why Terry, so distracted by the targeting system, didn't hit the mountain. (Be honest, you thought he was a goner.) When the system noticed that he was about to crash it pulled up and saved his life. In a sense, we found a technological way to automate willpower. Thanks to Auto G-Cas, Terry is alive and was able to join NASA flying multiple missions into space, including being the commander of the International Space Station. And do you know whose space base didn't blow up while they were in charge? That would be Terry's, because, unlike Darth Vader, he is a lovely guy who knows how to create psychological safety.

When people are overwhelmed, instead of expecting more from them, it is far more effective to have a system in place that prevents the issue from coming up. That's why we have spell-check, meeting reminders, and the Find My Phone app. The Air Force is already pushing the limits of what a person can do, so instead of trying to train the pilots to handle more, they installed the Auto G-Cas system to prevent the issue from coming up in the first place.

At a certain point, we each reach our limit, and the easiest way to handle better habits is an automatic system. If you aren't good at staying on time, create a rule that at each meeting there is a timekeeper with ultimate power—now it's not your problem. Can't sit yourself down to write a proposal? Don't beat yourself up. Instead hire a virtual assistant to dictate your proposals to and edit them for you.

So, how did I stop myself from becoming an occasional jerk? I needed to prevent the pattern from having a chance to unfold. I could have spent months or years in therapy getting to the root of my anger, with no real guarantee that my behavior would change, or I could just put a system in place. So, we created an anti-jerk policy:

1. No matter what goes wrong at the company, moving forward it is *my* fault. Not because I did it but because I defined our processes and policies. If I had a better system in place, it wouldn't have gone wrong.

2. When there is a problem, it is reported, but we don't try to understand the issue yet, so I have time to get over it.

3. If there are any immediate issues, something that needs solving right now, we get to work, ideally having no contact with the person I would be upset with.

4. When I do talk to people, I let enough time pass that I emotionally disconnect from the incident, and everyone from the team suggests ways that will prevent it from happening ever again.

Notice that we needed a process to prevent my bad reactions. It wasn't enough for me to say I wouldn't do it again. I needed rules to avoid the trigger point completely. As a result, any problem that comes up of any size is reported quickly, and I have a clear view of what is going on because my team feels safe.

So, what about Draymond? Obviously he needs to work on managing his emotions and anger, but his individual efforts could be supported by a new system. The easiest way to stop a bad habit is to not be in a situation where it comes up. What we want is an early warning system like we have for tsunamis and earthquakes; even five to ten seconds' notice would be enough to prevent him from getting too angry. Something as simple as wearing technology like an Apple Watch or a vitals tracker might be enough to see it coming and let the coach rotate him out for a minute to calm down. Notice that this system is completely passive; it creates no new work for anyone once it is created, and it can be used by any player.

What about Draymond's defenders, who suggest that part of what makes him so good is his willingness to cross the line and scare other players away? That it's okay for this particular star player to break the culture of the organization because he is so special. If your argument is that what makes basketball great is the violence, that's just a trash argument. If a team can't win by being better athletes, the answer isn't to win by injuring the other team. Making one exception destroys the values that the game is played on, and if violence is the answer then we should just watch MMA tournaments.

Ultimately, a good system at work can protect everyone and preserve the social contract. It can also ensure that the negative impact of people's weaker skills is diminished.

Getting In the Reps and Building the Muscle

The simple and annoying truth is that it is nearly impossible to develop a skill without putting in a lot of effort. You can't develop strong muscles without exercising them, you can't become a fantastic public speaker without spending time onstage and practicing, and you can't be a Formula 1 racer if you don't spend hours behind the wheel. But we have been misled about how mastery works.

In his book *Outliers*, Malcolm Gladwell asks what it takes to be masterful at a skill. He shares the story of an experiment lead by K. Anders Ericsson at a music school, where violinists were ranked based on skill and were asked how many hours they practiced alone. Note that it wasn't just any practice: it was concerted effort. What this means is that you can send your kid to play in a pool every day of the summer, but they might not become better swimmers. They will probably spend a lot of time in water fights, breath-holding competitions, running around with friends, and doing all the things kids do that annoy lifeguards. If they want to become better swimmers, they need to practice their strokes, do laps, examine their technique, and get feedback. Concerted effort is actively focused on the goal of improvement.

In most training at work, we are taught a skill once, with no follow-up. We skim a work manual, receive forty-five minutes of instruction, or binge a YouTube video on a skill we may have exaggerated on our resume, and hope no one calls us out on our incompetence. But with most skills, we need repeated practice with concerted effort. So, what did Ericsson's study find? Spoiler alert: top performers outpracticed everyone else, clocking in at about 10,000 hours over the course of their lifetime. The midrange violinists practiced a lot less and the lowest ranked even less. That's where Gladwell's claim comes from—that 10,000 hours is the magic number for mastery. He compares the hours of practice to an estimate of the hours that Bill Gates programmed before starting Microsoft with Paul Allen and the Beatles practiced together before becoming the band we know today.

This story spread the popularity of the so-called 10,000 hour rule, that anyone wanting professional-level skills just has to practice that many hours and they will be a superstar. Unfortunately, we have been completely misled. It's not as simple as anyone who clocks the practice time becomes a professional. If you practiced basketball for 10,000 hours, I'm sorry, but you would not be LeBron James. You would barely be good enough to be LeBron's towel person. There is a lot to unpack here, so let's start with the basics.

One issue with this theory is that it was one experiment, on one school, one time, and then it was turned into an internet meme. And although every other internet meme you have ever read is obviously true, this one has been debunked. Research led by Case Western Reserve University psychologist Brooke Macnamara did a meta-analysis looking at topics like sports, music, and education and found that "deliberate practice explained 26% of the variance in performance for games, 21% for music, 18% for sports, 4% for education, and less than 1% for professions. We conclude that deliberate practice is important but not as important as has been argued." I'm sorry to say, but I think the meme lied to us.

Let's look at chess, a skill that is known to require an extraordinary amount of dedication. The range of hours needed to qualify for a World Chess Federation title is as little as 3,000 hours to more than 20,000 hours of practice. That's almost seven times more practice between the low and high for the same qualification. It's no surprise that an idea this complex doesn't make a popular meme.

It also shouldn't surprise you that the number of hours is different depending on the skill you are trying to master. Being a professional violinist will clearly require more hours than being a world memory champion, pogo jumper, or extreme ironing champion (yes, that's a real thing). You can't standardize hours of practice and expect success.

We need to understand that practice is a part, and sometimes a very small part, of what causes us to be good at something, and although people tend to practice sports and skills, it seems almost no one ever puts in practice to develop career skills. You don't see Mike from accounting putting together PowerPoint decks to practice his storytelling skills or striking up a conversation at the water cooler to practice giving people feedback. So, should you practice if you want to improve? Yes, but you should also look at how to put the odds in your favor and what accounts for the other 74–99 percent of our ability to become great at something.

Match the Skill to Your Advantages

No doubt practice is essential to developing a skill, but genetics and other random advantages also play a major role in achieving mastery. As a personal example, I'm dyslexic. I was the last kid in my class to learn to read, and I still can't spell to save my life. It doesn't matter how many hours I practice spelling or what technique I use; I'm just not going to be a spelling bee champion. As a 5'10" guy in his forties I'm also not going to become a professional NBA player, but fun fact: one out of every ten people in the world who are seven feet tall play in the NBA. Clearly, genetics is a huge advantage.

The contrarians may point to a player like Muggsy Bogues at 5'3". I would argue that Muggsy was inch-for-inch the best player the NBA has ever had but, out of the several thousand players in NBA history, only one player was 5'3" and no one was ever shorter. Muggsy had to be so much more skilled than everyone else just to keep up with their genetic advantage.

We all love the story of someone overcoming the odds and accomplishing the seemingly impossible. It gives us hope, but there is a reason for that. For every Muggsy out there, there are thousands of delusional men playing pickup at the local YMCA and thinking that, with just a few more hours of practice, they could go pro. I'm not saying people should give up on their dreams—that's their call—but we want to go into the situation with open eyes. That same effort put into a skill where you have a natural advantage will catapult your results.

If we know we just aren't suited to something, we should stop beating ourselves up and either focus on something else or find a way around it. The good news is that in developing a business skill you don't need to be masterful or one of the best in the world; mostly we are just looking to be competent, the equivalent of just knowing how to dribble the ball in basketball. My workaround for being a bad speller is to work with an editor. I've also learned to embrace my natural strengths, which is why my style of writing sounds the way I talk. I don't try to sound like a great novelist, because I'm not one. Still, I can thrive as a writer in, arguably, a career I was never destined for.

So, when you look at skill development, ask yourself: Is this one worth developing in myself, or is it a skill that I could find in partnering with someone else or even in outsourcing it entirely? You might want to become a great storyteller; it doesn't mean you should be designing slides in PowerPoint, but as a storyteller you may want to practice presenting, watching great talks and learning from them, or telling stories at the Moth, an organization where people share "The Art and Craft of Storytelling." The key is in leaning into your advantages and finding a way to compensate for or automate the skills we will probably never be fantastic at. That may involve teaming up with someone who possesses strengths you don't have, taking on a coach or a mentor, or creating systems that boost your strength in these areas.

Mentorship and Coaching

Accomplishing anything extraordinary, especially strengthening skills and developing talent, isn't a solo act. As Allen Gannett points out in *The Creative Curve,* we are used to the idea of the lone genius creating great accomplishment, but great creatives like Beethoven and master chess players like Garry Kasparov practiced endlessly under masterful teachers. When Kasparov was seven, he went to a special school in Baku, in what was then the Azerbaijan Soviet Socialist Republic, and starting at age ten he was coached by incredible talents like Vladimir Makogonov, Alexander Nikitin, and Alexander Shakarov, to name a few. Without mentorship and coaching it is hard to spot our weaknesses and force ourselves to do the necessary work to improve. Can someone do it on their own? Maybe, but they will waste so much time and energy making mistakes that would never show up if you had a good coach or mentor.

Think about it like this: Pilots are taught the 1-in-60 rule, to keep them on track. Even though a mistake of one degree sounds like nothing, if you are just one degree off course, after 60 miles you will miss your goal by a mile. At the speed most commercial planes travel that would be missing your goal by about 9 or 10 miles the first hour. The longer you travel, the farther off course you are. A ten-hour flight would put you 90 to 100 miles off course. That's just one degree. You can imagine the same situation when someone is trying to improve on their own; the longer they work, the bigger the chance they have gone off course. Correcting for that later becomes harder and harder. A good coach or mentor will make sure you don't veer off course. They catch an error before it becomes a habit and make sure you practice and develop the right skills. And let's be honest, the added benefit of accountability increases the chances you will do the work.

So, what does the research say about coaching? One study found almost four times the productivity (measured by internal metrics) when people did training combined with eight weeks of coaching, versus those who just did training. According to research led by Gerald Olivero, "Training increased productivity by 22.4 percent. The coaching, which included goal setting, collaborative problem solving, practice, feedback, supervisory involvement, evaluation of end-results, and a public presentation, increased productivity by 88.0 percent, a significantly greater gain compared to training alone." A meta-analysis looking at twenty studies found that coaching at work has a huge impact on both accomplishing a goal and having the confidence to attempt it. The result was measured based on performance ratings, meaning coworkers and bosses thought people were more effective and achieved more when being coached. It's nice to have a coach who helps you believe in yourself, but when your coworkers and boss notice an improvement, that can have a big impact on your career. Obviously, not all coaches are great, but if you can develop a trusted relationship with someone good, they can really help you grow and develop.

Contagion

You might remember that at the beginning of the book I talked about one of my favorite studies of all time. It found that our behaviors are contagious, that if you have an obese friend, you are 45 percent more likely to be obese, your friends who don't know them have a 20 percent increase chance, and their friends have a 5 percent increase. By examining a large social network over thirty-two years, the researchers, Nicholas Christakis and James Fowler, were also able to see that this kind of effect is true for happiness, marriage and divorce rates, and smoking and voting habits. It means that just about any behavior is contagious through a social group.

How does this work? Well, if you are hanging out with a group of podcasters, and they are constantly talking about interviews, equipment, and audience growth, it is only a matter of time before you start thinking, Maybe I should have a show . . . If your coworker invites you to CrossFit and you make friends with other people in the class, and you stay in touch, chances are you too will develop a love for physical suffering in the name of self-improvement.

If you want to build a habit, it makes it a lot easier if you surround yourself with a lot of people who are competent or masterful at it. Instead of trying to build a skill from scratch, if you are socializing with people who are focused on it, the skill becomes contagious. You are constantly talking about it and learning from each other.

Obviously, this doesn't guarantee anything, but it does give you a real strategy: don't do it on your own, find the people who have the skill that you respect, and spend more time with them.

Your Attitude

Everything we covered so far is about what we can do, but we also need to touch on how we think. There are two parts to attitude, and one is a lot more ridiculous than the other.

The first should be straightforward. If you want to improve, be prepared to feel like an idiot and get a lot wrong along the way. Simply put, the difference between you and someone who has the skills is that they have probably already failed at what you are trying, learned the lesson, and improved. In the early days of running my Influencers Dinners, I was what would be technically referred to as a "hot mess." I was inviting people way more successful than I will ever be, and I never learned how to communicate with them. I would pitch an evening that appealed to a single twenty-nine-year-old, only to find (to my great shock!) that that was not the kind of party that appealed to a seventy-year-old Nobel Prize recipient. I would talk about it as the best party they could go to, and all they wanted to do was have a lovely evening talking to great people without straining to hear over loud dance music and my desperate need for approval. Having person after person saying "No, thank you, this isn't for me" sucked and I still cringe up, like I've bitten into a whole lemon, thinking about the failed attempts.

What successful, talented people often don't admit or talk about is that this awkward stage is unavoidable. Improving means mostly failing. I'm not going to pretend that I liked it, but it toughened me up and forced me to keep trying new approaches. Eventually I found a pitch that worked. Even now, I mess it up, but it doesn't sting as bad because I went through the awkward stage and got stronger. Put simply, "Embrace the suck."

The second part is way less predictable and far more absurd. Evidence suggests that if you want to improve to a professional level, you might need to be delusional. Here is what I mean. The percentage of Division 1 college athletes who thought it was at least "Somewhat likely" they would go pro is completely disconnected from reality.

SPORT	PERCEPTION	REALITY
Men's Basketball	76%	1.2%
Women's Basketball	44%	1.9%
Football	52%	1.6%
Baseball	60%	9.4%
Men's Ice Hockey	63%	0.8%
Men's Soccer	46%	1.9%

The numbers aren't even close. Only 1 out of every 63 D1 basketball players who think they have a shot make it to the NBA, which is an important caveat to my earlier claim that being delusional is a waste of time. It's only a waste of time most of the time. It reminds me of all the students at NYU at the same time as the Olsen twins who were convinced that, because they were in the same class, they had a shot at dating one of them. But here is the important point: the challenge of being a professional player is so hard and requires so much effort that you *have* to be delusional to think you can make it, or else no one would put the time in to begin with—between early morning practices, injuries and pain, the need to give up socializing and having fun—just to have a shot of playing at the professional level and hopefully bringing home a championship or a medal. It is decades of dedication. In other words, being a little or a lot delusion is probably a feature of those who excel. Still, you need more than a healthy dose of delusion to actually succeed at the highest levels—you need that and all the other elements I've described in this chapter.

The Military

In researching this book, I came across a lot references to the remarkable training and development that occurs in the military. Many consider it the gold standard, and often when we refer to great leaders, people share examples of military heroes. These leaders hold themselves to a standard we would never see in the workplace. They will risk their lives for their soldiers; meanwhile, in the corporate workplace, some people wouldn't skip their lunch break to help a coworker. So, what can we learn from the military about the things they do well? How do they create a profound trust and camaraderie that causes people to outperform?

- ***Continuous growth:*** Constant training and development are at the heart of all military branches, starting at a military academy or boot camp and continuing each time they receive a new rank. This continues all the way to the very top at the Joint Chiefs of Staff. The expectation is to grow both physically and mentally. Throughout a 25+ year career, a soldier will have thousands of hours of practice and training and certifications, both in the field and classroom. The culture supports growth and development in every aspect. This might mean anything from paratrooping and medical training to staying current on equipment maintenance standards. The people mentoring and coaching are actually subject matter experts; they often have real-world experience or at the very least certifications of competence in the area. They have often spent years specializing in that skill. Compare that to someone who graduates from college and, besides the on-the-job training they get when they start, the only other development they may get every year is watching a sexual harassment training video filmed in the 1980s, or a subscription to a meditation app. The military promotes a growth mindset; its members know there is no perfection, only a process toward mastery. People can experiment and try something, and if it fails, they can try something else next time, but there is always an opportunity for muscle-building.

- *Joint training and development:* When a commander is leading their people on a mission or training, they are there on the ground with them. They are part of the team, participating in the same activities no matter how difficult. When someone is suffering alongside you, working harder than everyone else, you may not like them, but you will respect them. The integration of leadership into the team creates greater trust and camaraderie. It causes people to feel more connected and invested in one another and can set higher expectations on the leader to set an example. When bullets are firing you learn quickly who can handle the burden of leadership.

- *Real feedback and development:* Each year everyone on a team provides a report on their commander, sharing the good and the bad. In response, the commander needs to provide a plan for tackling their areas of improvement. Status is then rewarded to those who make the effort to improve. Consider, on the other hand, that many people stay at a company for only two or three years at a time. This means there is no incentive to improve because there is no permanent record or culture to support growth. But in the military, if you want to earn status and rank, you will need the support of the people who report to you, and you will need to produce a clear growth strategy. Ultimately, they are rewarded for growth, competence, and only if people will follow them.

- *Healthy competition:* Team members may compete on speed, accuracy, skill level, etc., but the shared goal is clear: fulfill the mission, so everyone comes home safe and sound. They are not competing against each other but *with* each other against the enemy. We can see the healthy contagion of skills and expectations at work. When your life may depend on the person next to you, you are incentivized to make sure both that they are competent, and that you learn anything you can from them. The more capable the people around you are, the more you are rewarded with mission success, promotion, and, oh yeah, the ability to live another day. Meanwhile, in the corporate world, it tends to be more of a zero-sum game: you are rewarded more when the people around you are incompetent because you will get the performance bonus and the status.

- *Placement and roles:* The corporate world hires for a specific role, and that role might change during a career at a company. The military has the opposite process. Someone signs up and then they are placed in a role. This means that the objective is to get the person into the role that best matches their skill set. Clearly, at the scale of two million people, this is a challenging process, but it does mean that if you have a genetic or social advantage for specific roles, there is a good chance you will be pushed in the right direction. It's no surprise that so many Olympic swimmers become Navy SEALs, because they have the genetics and training to operate in those conditions, and if you are more tech-oriented you can be trained in cyberwarfare. This means there is a better chance of matching a person's gifts with a role where they can perform well.

You can see that the military has many of the characteristics that we outlined as important for growth and development: constant training, muscle-building, social contagion of skills, competent mentorship/coaching, and enough tenure to allow skill-building to occur. Does this mean they get it all right? Absolutely not, and they would be the first to admit it, and that's because they are always seeking to improve. For the military, what is at stake is people's lives and the safety of our democracy, so they don't have the privilege of being satisfied with the status quo; the culture needs continuous improvement so that they are always prepared.

Clearly, the business world operates with different priorities, and so we can't expect the culture to support you in the same ways. Instead individuals need to be far more proactive. We need to take the ideas in the chapter and apply them to any skill we want to improve.

What we know so far is that leadership is about followers, and people follow because you have some super skills that are so disproportionately strong that when people interact with them, they feel like there is a new future.

So, What's Next?

If you are going to work on your skills or habits, you will have the biggest gains from preventing the ones that breach the social contract, those that have a negative impact. After that, I would focus on getting a coach, since the process of finding one will be faster than a lot of other options. Or I would look at how to enjoy the benefits of contagion, not because it is more important than the others, but because making friends and socializing has a lot of other benefits, and your immersion into a skill will happen more naturally.

As an intelligent and critical reader, you have probably noticed that until now we have only explored what makes a leader. In the next chapters we will explore how you maximize your team's intelligence and unlock its collective genius.

Ideas in Action

- Since psychological safety is such a critical component for creating effective teams, the biggest area of improvement may be in preventing breaches of the social contract rather than having small improvements in other skills.

- Telling ourselves we won't repeat a bad habit is unrealistic. Instead we are better off creating a system that stops any issues before they come up.

- To improve there are several critical strategies:
    - *Get ready to practice:* Be prepared to practice a lot and to fail in the process. The difference between you and someone who is masterful is that they have pushed through more failures. Muscle-building is important, but it isn't the only factor that matters.
    - *Lean on your genetic advantages:* We all have natural advantages, and trying to go against them reduces your chances of success. Find ways to apply your advantages to the skills you are developing, and outsource the rest as best you can.
    - *Social contagion:* Surround yourself with people who have the skill you admire, and chances are it will more naturally become part of your habits, conversations, and practice.
    - *Get a coach:* A good coach will both accelerate your development and prevent you from going off course.

Part II

Teams—Unlocked

Chapter 4
Welcome to the Team

Unless you are a flatworm and reproduce asexually, meaning you are basically born pregnant and have babies on your own, then you are going to need to work as part of a team at least once (but probably a lot more) to prevent our species from dying out.

A person trying to be annoying might say that someone can live alone, work remotely, and never contact other people, and I hope you would agree that is just a dumb argument. When that person wants to work remotely, they need a computer made by thousands of people. If they want to eat, a team needs to grow and deliver the supplies. When they need medical attention, a team will be involved in their care. Everything we touch is made through team effort, including us. The argument for full self-reliance is stupid.

You want more proof? When we think of Neanderthals (aka cavemen), we often imagine stupid versions of humans, but it turns out that they were stronger than us and at least as smart. So why did we survive, and they didn't? This should be obvious by now: we live in large communities of about 150 people versus Neanderthals' small groups of fifteen or so. Humans' superpower may very well be our instinct to form large communities. For human beings, being part of a team is essential to survival.

Now for a quick and shameless plug: As I pointed out in my last book, *You're Invited* (you should buy a copy or twelve), anything that matters to people is a by-product of who we are connected to, how much they trust us, and the level of belonging we feel. In the book I shared research that shows if you want to predict how long someone will live, look at the number of close friends they have and how many people they connect with in a day. If you want to predict business success like company stock value, employee sick days, and profitability, just look at the level of trust in a company. If you want to look at team success, it stems from psychological safety.

Maybe you want to die young, have a low stock value, or have a team that fears you: Sure, Neanderthal, just focus on yourself. But did you know that if you're starting a company, having a cofounder increases your chances of getting an investment by more than 30 percent, multiplies your growth rate, and reduces the chances you will scale too fast?

And so we've come back to one of the main themes of this book: that the smallest unit of effectiveness at work is a team. This means our goal should be to maximize team intelligence.

Are there exceptions? Sure, but those people aren't likely to be reading this book anyway. So, let's take a look at what my sociable, smart readers should know.

Trickle-Down Leadership

So far, the business world has focused on a waterfall or trickle-down leadership strategy. If I invest in training and developing the people at the top, the results will trickle down to everyone. There is a logic to it. The people at the top have the highest paychecks and the most decision-making power, so we want them to be operating at their best.

Unfortunately, this strategy means that if you have one leader along the way who misses the training or doesn't know how to communicate an idea, that weak link can have a huge negative impact on the rest of the organization. Luckily, corporate America is so good at hiring, and training people, that I can't imagine that would ever be a problem.

If we are really honest, many promotions don't go to the people who would be the best leaders or instructors, but to the people who are good at managing up, meaning they communicate well with their bosses, or they are good enough at their job (for example, they were the top salesperson, and thus they should be the sales manager, even though those skills are completely different).

It's the Peter principle at work. The basic idea is that in a hierarchy, people will keep getting promoted until they can't do their jobs anymore. Let me explain: If someone joins a company and is doing a fantastic job, they will get a promotion, and maybe another, and another, but at a certain point they just don't shine as bright in their new role. At the point when they don't have the skill to go any further, they get stuck. Essentially they started out capable of doing their work and kept getting promoted until they were incompetent—only now, guess what, they're your boss. Awesome! If they had the skill to shine at this job, they would have probably been promoted to be your boss's boss, but they don't, and now you know why so many people think so little of their boss.

When Laurence J. Peter wrote *The Peter Principle* in 1969, it was just something he noticed, but a team of researchers from the University of Minnesota, MIT, and Yale looked at more than 53,000 sales employees at 214 American companies, and the results were comedic. There were two important insights. Of the 1,500 or so sales reps who were promoted to sales manager:

1. The best salespeople were more likely to be promoted.

2. These best salespeople performed poorly as managers.

Just because you are really good at one job doesn't mean your skills transfer to another role. Said another way, just because I'm good at eating Cheetos does not mean I should be the next CEO of Frito-Lay.

We have all had the experience that if a job is too easy, we find it boring and we are disengaged. If it is way too hard, then we can crumble from the stress. We generally want the Goldilocks zone, where we are competent enough to do the work, but still feel like it is new and different enough that we can learn and grow. It's the excitement of improvement and new opportunities (and frankly, the recognition of that improvement from our boss, colleagues, and work crush) that tends to keep us engaged. But there is a difference between being able to do the work while still growing and being incompetent. We don't have to start out being great at our job, but we probably can't suck at it either. This isn't Little League.

Regardless, we need to accept that in a waterfall or trickle-down hierarchy, each additional layer of management and leadership can potentially ease stress by reducing how many people report to someone, but it is also another point of confusion. Any messaging, strategy, and culture from the top leadership of the company now must filter through even more people in what often looks like a game of broken telephones.

So now we have a problem. To accomplish anything big we need other people, and the bigger the goal, the more people we generally need. But when we focus only on the leaders, it tends not to work. At the beginning of this book, I shared that about $40 billion a year is spent on leadership training and there is no evidence that it has any long-term impact. You probably spent at most thirty bucks on this book, and I'd love for it to have an impact.

So, in the face of all this, what do we focus on?

To answer that question, I started by looking at a painfully long experiment that began at 11:15 a.m. on July 7, 1919. That morning, eighty-one vehicles left the White House in Washington, DC, with a mission to arrive in San Francisco. Heading west, they arrived at the Frederick Fairgrounds in Maryland, forty-six miles away, a mere seven hours later. After sleeping for the night, they packed up and repeated the process, traveling forty to sixty miles day, one after another.

Yes, you read that right: they were driving about fifty miles each day. Going through the Appalachian Mountains, then through Ohio, and crossing the Mississippi River, they struggled at every stage. As if it weren't hard enough to drive those old vehicles through mud and mountains, at least there were gas stations and clear roads. But the farther west they went, the fewer supplies they could find; it was barren. The trip across the country had to be planned like an expedition across Antarctica, carrying anything they could need (food, water, gas, etc.). One participant later wrote, "In those days, we were not sure it could be accomplished at all. Nothing of the sort had ever been attempted."

Their plan may have been to take the Lincoln Highway across the country, but it was in such bad shape that they would often need to find alternate routes. Let's not forget that when they would reach covered bridges, their vehicles would be too big, and parts of the bridges would need to be taken apart. In many places, they would be lucky if there was a bridge at all, and when the road narrowed to a single lane, they would need to manage oncoming traffic with their eighty-one-vehicle lineup. In 1919, a highway didn't exactly look the way it does now. Think more of a beaten-down dirt road than the smooth pavement we know today. As they approached California, conditions improved, the roads were paved, and they were able to reach San Francisco on September 6, 1919, a mere sixty-two days after leaving the White House. When I used to play the Oregon Trail computer game in elementary school, I lost dozens of virtual souls to dysentery and snake bites, but even those ill-fated expeditions didn't take sixty-two days.

On average, they traveled at 5.65 miles an hour. To put that in perspective, ultramarathon runner Pete Kostelnick set the record for running across the US in forty-two days. The reason anyone would torture themselves with a two-month treacherous drive through mud, mountains, and barren land wasn't for the thrill of adventure. After World War I, the US military wanted to understand how realistic it would be to get across the country. Is it possible for military trucks and supplies to reach the places they need to get to? As you would have guessed, the report was terrible; essentially it was almost impossible unless roads improved. There was no safe way for the military to transport people, supplies, vehicles, and equipment across the US roadways, and it was a matter of national security.

This is why, at the time, most people preferred the comfort and speed of a passenger train. No one in their right mind would drive across the country unless it was a publicity stunt. It was true that some states had built great local road systems, especially near the major cities, but the states were mostly disconnected from each other, and they didn't see the point in spending state funds to fix a federal issue.

As more Americans bought cars, and society became more dependent on fast transportation, people dreamed of an Interstate Highway System that would allow not just the military to function and people to travel, but for supplies to be traded between states, crops to be transported quickly without spoiling, and a chain of fast-casual restaurants to bring southern comfort food to the whole nation. It would take another world war to inspire a solution (and the dream of a Cracker Barrel at every exit was also more than a generation away).

During World War II, US and European forces led by Supreme Allied Commander General Dwight D. Eisenhower experienced Germany's national Reichsautobahn. This four-lane highway system was so efficient that when German forces were retreating after D-Day, Allied forces were able to get onto the Reichsautobahn and get ahead of the Germans using their own roads. They were elevated and incredibly engineered, so even tanks could maneuver on them at speed.

After the war, Eisenhower served as Army chief of staff under President Harry Truman and became the first supreme commander of NATO. On November 4, 1952, he was elected president of the United States, winning in a landslide victory.

Now in office, Eisenhower had to pave the way for the future of the country, and I mean that quite literally. He believed that for the US to thrive the answer lay in having a German-style highway system. It didn't matter how good US soldiers or military technology was if we couldn't get them where and when we needed them. Major cities like New York, Chicago, San Francisco, and Dallas can't thrive without being able to transport in things like agricultural, timber, and metal. Farms can't succeed if they are limited to customers near the local roadways, or if there is no way to get equipment to them. A family can't thrive if their dad can't pile the kids into the back of their Subaru and hit seven national parks in ten days like the Founding Fathers intended. A society lives and dies by its ability to connect, trade, travel, and get resources where they need to be as efficiently as possible.

The same is true for teams. As we've seen, an effective team isn't created by staffing it only with superstars; we increase team intelligence when there are strong connections between members. Can the talent effectively communicate, and transfer resources and information, or are their connections to each other like the 1919 US roadway, constantly having problems, unclear about how to get past them, and taking months to accomplish something that should take a few days?

What Eisenhower knew was that in a country with so much potential, the most important way to unlock and protect it would be to increase the connections between resources. The truth is he had probably been planning this idea for thirty-three years. As a young lieutenant colonel, he participated in the 1919 cross-country military convoy. The quote you read a few paragraphs back, about not knowing if the team would make it across the country, was his. He knew firsthand how disconnected the country was, and now, having seen the strength and potential of an Interstate Highway System, he knew his mission. For the next several years he worked to bring to life the Federal-Aid Highway Act of 1956, dedicating about $25 billion to his dream, but the story doesn't end there.

It's important to understand that when attempting to connect, the unexpected eventually happens. In the case of the US highway system, since they were creating a national standard that would support both trade and the military, it went through mountains, not around them; roads were straight so planes could land on them; and highways, unlike surface roads, were elevated so tanks could drive on them. By the late 1960s the budget had already doubled and only about 60 percent of the highways were built, but the impact was already incredible. Denver had doubled its population and Houston had tripled. Meanwhile, Phoenix had grown ten times larger. Towns like Albuquerque and Dallas became major cities.

When people and resources are transported easily, it unlocks potential. Through an absolute marvel of modern engineering, construction teams were able to tunnel through the Rocky Mountains, connecting the West Coast to the rest of the country. In 1992, thirty-six years after the project began, the last section was built. Unfortunately, Eisenhower wasn't alive to see it, but his dream lived on through the incredible prosperity and military security the US achieved through its highway system. Altogether the project cost $114 billion (equivalent to $597 billion in 2022).

This story exemplifies one of the most important lessons of teams. You can have great people, but your potential won't be realized until the connections between individuals and their unique talents and resources are brought together. The processes to connect them will probably take longer and require more resources than you plan, but the result will be a team that can operate at its best, where resources and communication can flow effectively.

In case you were curious, in the mid-1970s an unsanctioned cross-country race known as the Cannonball Run began putting the coast-to-coast challenge to the test. As of October 2021 the trip time has reduced from 62 days to just over a day (25 hours and 39 minutes—at an average speed of 113 miles an hour), driven by Arne Toman and Doug Tabbutt.

Don't Go Chasing Waterfalls

There are definitely times when a top-down waterfall system can be effective, especially in an emergency, but it's not great for everything. Imagine if every city only had one road that went directly to Washington, DC. Now resources could flow to and from the president faster, but it would create an absolute mess. Every time I needed something from another city it would have to travel to DC first. Yet in organizations we design a ridiculous system where managers and leaders have to go through their boss for every little thing. That's what the waterfall system does: it makes us swim upstream to get anything done.

But there is another option. We can rethink the entire purpose of leaders and managers. When sports fans talk about the great coaches in history, they often think the coach succeeded because of their strategic thinking, work ethic, or brilliant training approach. In sports movies and shows they always pan across boards with Xs and Os on them showing how everyone should move. That's what a coach does: he tells the Xs and Os where to go, like a chess master positioning their pieces to win the match.

But according to data scientists and bestselling author Seth Stephens-Davidowitz, "When you compare NBA coaches, talent of their players, and performance, the greatest predictor of the positive impact of a coach is how much more their players pass when they have that coach."

At first, this might sound stupid. From what people tell me, you don't get points in basketball for passing as many times as possible, but for throwing the ball into a metal circle dressed beautifully with a little net on it. As you can tell, I know almost nothing about basketball. Passing is so important because, if a player only cares about himself, he will take as many shots as he can. But, crucially, if the player trusts the team and cares about the group's results, he will pass more often so the ball can get to the person that is in the best position to score—so long as the person in the best position to score is not me, lifelong benchwarmer Jon Levy.

You can practice passing every day, but if the players don't feel a sense of connection and trust with each other, on game day they will focus on themselves. Great coaches make the players feel connected to one another, create a sense of belonging, and contribute to everyone's success. This is why if a player goes from passing 30 percent of the time to 55 percent, what it really tells us is that not only are they more focused on the team's success, but chances are that the coach is really great at creating a sense of team. They are putting in the work to maximize team intelligence.

I should point out that there has been one other metric that relates to successful teams: they touch more. A team of researchers led by Michael W. Kraus coded all the physical contact between teammates in the 2008 regular season and found that "early season touch predicted greater performance for individuals as well as teams later in the season. Additional analyses confirmed that touch predicted improved performance even after accounting for player status, preseason expectations, and early season performance."

This shouldn't surprise us; you don't want to have physical contact with people you dislike, unless maybe it's your fist contacting their nose, so when physical contact is welcome it demonstrates warmth, belonging, and trust. Obviously, when we translate this finding to an office setting, we can probably agree that a high five or a fist bump might be okay, but a lot of other forms of touch the researchers saw, such as "chest bumps, leaping shoulder bumps, chest punches, head slaps, head grabs," etc. probably aren't great for the office.

What Eisenhower understood and Seth Stephens-Davidowitz saw in NBA data is that the job of a leader is to unlock the intelligence of their team by ensuring that they are connected to each other in a meaningful, trusting way. In other words, like my third-grade teacher told my mother: "Jon needs to learn to work and play well with others."

In waterfall leadership, we hope that if we pass a leader information, they are good enough at commanding their people that they can solve a problem. The leader functions as a hub were everything flows through to ensure a solution is reached. It is exhausting and prevents the team from working quickly. In the opening of this book, I pointed out that if a leader has nine reports, in a waterfall model we are only looking at those nine relationships. Instead, in a connection model we understand that between ten team members (the leader included) there are forty-five relationships, and that's where the magic happens.

A great coach/leader ensures that people are connected to each other already. This allows them to use their talents to solve problems in real time, without prompting, and most effectively.

It should be obvious that most of the work done by a team doesn't involve the manager, so unless they hire incompetent people, or the manager has trust problems, why would everything have to flow through the manager? Instead, like a sports team or a country, the magic is unlocked thanks to the strength of the relationships between the cities and people so that interactions can move quickly and effectively.

I want to emphasize a few important points. The first is that you might be thinking, Jon, I have a lot of skills, and some are fantastic super skills that have inspired people to follow me, but I'm just not a people person. And to that I will say, there are a lot of people who don't have an easy time with the social parts of work, like Paul Erdős, the mathematician from Chapter 2; Apple cofounder Steve Wozniak; Marie Curie, who received two Nobel Prizes; and Abraham Lincoln, whom you may have heard of. They all struggled with the social aspects. So you are in good company, and it's not a deal breaker by any means. You can always pick up new skills and improve. But you can also accept that it doesn't always need to be you. You can have someone on the team who is fantastic at creating connections and culture, and you can task them with playing that role (while you work on improving your own skills). Even the best coaches have assistant coaches that have super skills they don't.

So, if we are only going to focus on one thing as a team leader, it should be making sure that the connections and trust between team members are strong enough to get the work done. As a reminder from Chapter 3, the breaches of the social contract have a much greater negative impact than the positives have a benefit. Once you tackle those, you want to understand how to connect people and create belonging.

In no place has that been proven better than in research done on high school popularity by Mitch Prinstein. Being popular has two parts: status (being admired or feared) and likability. High status is about how powerful or dominant we are, like the stereotypical attractive/rich kid, the bully, or mean girl cheerleader. Notice they often break the social contract. These people are often disliked by their peers, and things don't tend to turn out well for them. They have higher rates of relationship difficulties, anxiety, depression, and addiction, and are less likely to keep their jobs. Meanwhile, likability is based on how much we make others feel happy, valued, and included. It is an essential ingredient too in healthy groups and organizations. The students who are most likable have two traits: they connect with a lot of classmates from different groups regardless of social status, and they show those classmates that they like them. If our interactions make you feel that you belong, wouldn't you like me more? That's why likable people are hired and promoted more, make more money, and have higher happiness and fulfillment in their lives. Being likable isn't about me desperately wanting your approval. I'm not trying to fill some infinite void of insecurity by getting you to like me. Instead, it is about me showing you that you are valued and connected. What it keeps coming back to is that people are at their best when they feel connected and part of the group.

The Fast Lane to Connection and Trust

At this point, I've made the case that stronger connections are better, and that trust is essential to team intelligence. But what exactly do I mean by trust?

What Trust Is Made Of

When we look at what trust is made of, we see three things. In order of importance:

- *Benevolence:* The other person has your best interests at heart.

- *Honesty:* They are truthful and act with integrity.

- *Competence:* They are capable of doing the job that is expected of them.

Sadly, much of what we do in the corporate world to connect and build trust has the opposite effect. You will notice that unless your boss is a Bond villain, a breach in competence is easily forgiven. For example, when someone who is usually good at pitching messes up a presentation once, it is generally chalked up to a bad day. But if you find out that someone has been lying to you, you likely won't trust them, because a single lie is much worse than a single messed-up presentation.

Now imagine you are walking with a friend, and they need to quickly grab something they forgot at home, but when you arrive it is your surprise party. Yes, they lied, but for your benefit; they deceived you for benevolent reasons. It would be strange to hold that against them. Meanwhile, a breach in benevolence, like when your doctor is getting kickbacks for prescribing you drugs, is considered the most heinous. Even if the doctor tells us they're in the pockets of Big Pharma, we don't thank them for their honesty: we get a new doctor. Fundamentally we value benevolence, then honesty, and then competence. Yet most of corporate communication leads with competence, from our sales presentations and team communication to one-on-one feedback. We try to show our expertise (competence) rather than demonstrating that we understand and care for the other person's success and results (benevolence). It's no surprise that so little communication lands effectively.

You want another example of how we get it wrong? It is very common to invite potential customers to business dinners, but when you survey people on how much they enjoy those, you get about a 3 out of 10 unless they know each other ahead of time. The reason is that it's really tough to buy a relationship. It's like saying, "I know you don't like my personality, but I have concert tickets to your favorite musician. Do you want to go out?" Basically, we are trying to rent people's time, in hopes that they will like us. Instead, here are the things that really work.

The Ikea Effect

People care more about their Ikea furniture because they have to assemble it. And because that furniture inspired the single greatest fight of their relationship—a crucible of pegs, pins, and POÄNG that tested their love to the limit, only to come out stronger and more committed on the other side. Anything we put effort into we care more about, from our pets and kids to projects. Instead of trying to buy a relationship, find ways for employees to invest effort into one another. This will cause them to care more. We often accomplish this through playing games, doing activities, or having meaningful conversations, like "How many times did you consider filing for divorce after going with your spouse to Ikea?"

Stacking

When researchers stopped strangers and asked them for complex directions, people rarely helped, but when they first asked for the time, and then the directions, they almost always got the directions. Once someone has done us a small favor, they are more likely to do us a larger favor. We are often worried about bothering people, but being on a team means we will occasionally need people's help; that's not a bad thing, it's healthy. If you want to bond a team, start with finding small, supportive actions team members can help each other with. Let the Ikea effect kick in a bit, and then they will feel comfortable asking for the big help. It's like that Bill Withers song, "Lean on Me." "When you're not strong, I'll be your friend. I'll help you feel more comfortable in the workplace, allowing you to be more efficient and productive, making my job easier, everyone's job easier, and the company more successful!" Ah, the lyrics just roll off the tongue!

Vulnerability Loops

The smallest unit of trust is called a vulnerability loop. Most people think that if we are trustworthy, people will be vulnerable with us. It turns out the situation is the other way around. *Because* we are vulnerable, people trust us. It happens in a predictable five-stage process:

- **Person 1: Signals vulnerability**—"I am a little nervous for my big presentation. Can I get your feedback?"

- **Person 2: Acknowledges**—"Of course, I would be happy to."

- **Person 2: Signals vulnerability back to the same degree**—"I know how you feel, I was super nervous before my first big presentation."

- **Person 1: Acknowledges**—"Thank you so much for your help and understanding."

- **Both Person 1 and 2** see they are safe at this higher level of vulnerability, so trust increases.

Vulnerability precedes trust. So, if we want to build trusting teams, we need to do two things:

1. *Be on the lookout for when people signal vulnerability:* If a team member signals vulnerability (that is, asks for help, expresses anxiety about a pending task) and we don't close the loop by showing concern or providing assistance—if we instead make fun of them or insult them—trust is reduced.

2. *Be the first to signal:* Often it falls on the leader to start a vulnerability loop. But start small. I wouldn't recommend saying on your first day, "My marriage is falling apart, my

restless-leg syndrome keeps me up at night, and I just cried and threw up in the bathroom—because I'm nervous for my first presentation, not because of the leg or relationship stuff." Maybe a little too vulnerable, right? Try a smaller vulnerability first: ask someone for advice, like feedback on a talk, strategy, or even a gift for a loved one, and work your way up, just like with stacking.

The Pratfall Effect

All too often, we believe that if we look perfect, people will trust us more. I don't know about you, but when most of us meet someone who presents as perfect, it makes us feel insecure. Or we know it's all a facade, and they're hiding something (wait, do they also have restless-leg syndrome?). We now know that vulnerability precedes trust.

Researchers put this to the test. People were sent to interviews and either delivered a perfect interview or "accidentally" spilled some coffee or dropped some papers. When the reviews came in, those who spilled and dropped outranked those who were perfect. I know, you thought those kinds of antics only worked in rom-com meet-cutes, but it could actually land you your dream job.

When we can demonstrate vulnerability without damaging our credibility (you did the coffee spill bit but, oh no, you were interviewing for a job at Starbucks!), people like and trust us more.

Finding Common Ground

A nation connects through highways, but people tend to connect over common ground. We tend to trust, and like, things that are familiar. In fact, in one study some colleagues and I ran on 421 million potential matches on the dating app Hinge, we found that across almost every characteristic, opposites do not attract. This is just another popular dating myth, like playing hard to get or every kiss begins with *k*. Kiss in Spanish is *beso*, you fools! The more similar you are, the more likely you are to date down to your initials. If you have the same initials, you are 11.3 percent more likely to date. That trend flips once you get to having the same grandparents, unless you're a Targaryen from *Game of Thrones* or from certain states. We all know the ones I'm talking about.

For people to connect, it helps for them to find their common ground as quickly as possible around four elements: friends, culture, interest, and activities.

On my site www.JonLevy.com, I provide several free exercises that you can run with your team to help bond them in as little as five or ten minutes. One quick example is Get to Know You Bingo, where after splitting people into teams of four or five, if any two people on the team have the same answer to a prompt on the board, they mark it off. The first team to get five in a row wins, but more importantly you discover all the common ground people have quickly. This is just a starting point so you can create the trust needed to help your team increase its intelligence.

Ideas in Action

- Humans are at their best when they are part of a high-functioning team.

- More connections create better access to resources and new opportunities for everyone involved.

- If you can get people to pass the ball more—that is, collaborate more and share resources more frequently—team success will increase. But that depends on trust.

- High status might impress in the short run, but likability is what creates sustainable working relationships.

- Trust has three ingredients: benevolence, honesty, and competence, in order of importance.

- To get people to connect more deeply, find ways for them to invest effort in each other (the Ikea effect), and open and close vulnerability loops.

Chapter 5
Super Chickens (The Too-Much-Talent Problem)

It should be clear by now that the world has focused far too much on the leader's ability to lead, and far too little on the team's ability to . . . what's the word . . . *team*? So, if we want to succeed, both as a leader and as a team member, the key is to get the best talent we can and connect them around a common goal. Okay, there you have it! That's our show folks, thank you and good night!

It may sound simple enough, yet when researchers looked at the performance of high-talent teams, they found a frustrating and unexpected relationship between skill and success. More talent initially helped to a point, but when top talent made up more than about 50–60 percent of the team, the teams became less effective. This is known as the too-much-talent problem. We all know that too much of a good thing can be harmful, whether it's sunlight, exercise, or self-help books. A research team led by Roderick I. Swaab asked the question, Is there an upper limit to talent across different sports? They found that when European football teams competing in the World Cup have more than 60 percent top talent, they underperform and score fewer goals.

In basketball, NBA teams with more than 50 percent top talent (players with stats in the top third) also underperform. It might be tempting to read this and say, great, I'm going to hire 50 percent stars and a bunch of average employees to my team, and we will have peak performance. But before we jump to any conclusions, we want to understand why this happens, and we need to find counterexamples.

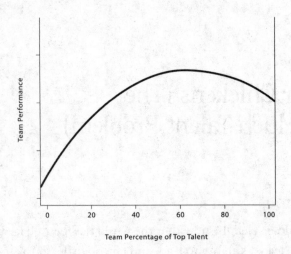

Team Percentage of Top Talent

Are there situations where *more* talent consistently leads to better results? Fortunately, the researchers repeated their study on baseball and found no upper limit. The proof is in the pinstripes. For decades the Yankees have packed their team with as many stars as their deep pockets could afford, and as of writing this, they have won the World Series twenty-seven times, nearly triple that of any other team.

Maybe these are just exceptions, or maybe what we are seeing is less to do with talent and more to do with the sport (or workplace). And that's exactly what the researchers found. What defined the maximum amount of talent was the level of "task interdependence." The more the team members have to interact with each other, and the more their work depends on one another, the less important maximizing individual talent becomes. A single-person activity like public speaking, driving, or working on an assembly line might not depend much on others; it's more like playing singles tennis or chess. Having more talent has a positive impact on outcomes. Meanwhile, during a World Cup football match, the players are constantly coordinating and passing the ball between each other, and in basketball, with only five people on the court from each team, the players' "task interdependence" is incredibly high. So why does baseball defy this rule? Baseball is an individual sport pretending to be a team sport. Almost none of the players interact with each other. If you are batting, you are all alone; if you are an outfielder, you aren't interacting with the catcher.

What this means is that if you are leading a team that has no reason to interact with each other ever, then you don't have to worry about the too-much-talent problem. But let's be honest, that's just not how most work happens. Besides the corporate softball league, almost anything anyone works on these days requires group collaboration, and that means high task interdependence, which means that talent alone is not the right stuff to launch you into the stratosphere of success.

Super Chickens vs. Super Teams

William Muir is an evolutionary biologist with an incredible drive to help us feed people more effectively and ethically. He has dedicated his life to chickens. Initially, you might think that's strange, but the world loves eating chickens. Whatever number of these birds you think are born (much less eaten) in a year, you are way off. I was shocked to find out that the world consumes an estimated 74 billion chickens a year.

When Muir started his work in 1983, the premier commercial chicken, the Dekalb XL, was bred generation after generation for pure productivity; it could outlay any chicken out there. These super chickens were amazingly effective, but when you bred for pure productivity, an unexpected side effect was that the chickens became incredibly aggressive. They were known for pecking each other to death or even turning to cannibalism. Let's just say there was a lot of fowl play.

To try to prevent this, farms started trimming these birds' beaks. Yes, it is as awful as it sounds. You can see why Muir wanted to find a more ethical way to feed people, one where he bred chickens that were both productive (laid a lot of eggs) and social (nonviolent or cannibalistic).

He started with standard crossbred chickens. They weren't special in any way whatsoever, and instead of putting them in individual cages, he created two hundred, nine-chicken teams, with each team living communally in a cage. Remember, these chickens had to be social, so instead of breeding for individual productivity, he wanted to know which team would produce the most pounds of eggs. After one year, he took the top twenty teams and used them to breed a new generation of two hundred teams so he could repeat the process. After six generations he had bred Kinder Gentler Birds, or the KGB, as he jokingly referred to them, because they didn't peck at each other; they just laid a lot of eggs. Fundamentally Muir had created super teams that had incredible productivity and prosocial behavior.

It wasn't enough for his chickens to be good citizens. For Muir to have an impact on the industry, they needed to be better than any other option. So, Muir ran two competitions. At the same time he was breeding the super teams, he also kept a control group of the original crossbred chickens he had started with. He wanted to know, if he selected one chicken from the super team and compared its egg-laying output to a chicken from the control group, would there be a difference?

The answer surprised him: there was no noticeable difference in productivity between the individual chickens. You would think this was a failure, but when the prosocial chicken went back with its teammates, the team outproduced the control group. After six generations these chickens were better together than apart; somehow these super teams were greater than the sum of their parts.

It seems at last we know why the chicken crossed the road: she wanted to find better labor conditions on the other side. Can you tell by that dad joke I had another child while writing this book?

Muir had one more competition ahead of him. How would his super team compare to a *team* of Dekalb XL super chickens? He put them beak-to-beak, a twelve-chicken super team, against a group of twelve super chickens. This was a winner-take-all challenge that could redefine the industry. If Muir's chickens won, he would have proved that we can feed more people in a more humane way. If his super team lost, it would mean the industry would have no reason to reconsider its practices.

After a year of competition, the numbers were in. Muir's super team beat the industry-standard Dekalb XL super chickens by a massive amount. By the end of the experiment, only three of the super chickens remained alive. The rest had been pecked to death. So, which came first, the chicken or the egg? Well, it turns out the answer is neither if your chickens are antisocial sociopaths. Meanwhile, Muir's super team was healthy, well feathered, and continuing to produce. After almost a decade of research, Muir had accomplished what his industry saw as impossible; he managed to breed for both productivity and sociability. His research confirmed that great teams not only beat superstars but also outlast them.

As an evolutionary biologist, Muir knew that any traits that are rewarded through continued breeding will thrive. He didn't need to subject his chickens to personality tests or send them off to a leadership retreat. Instead, he relied on group selection theory. All he had to do was keep rewarding the teams that succeeded for working together as a team. If the chickens were alive, healthy, and outproduced as a team, they would be selected to breed. The following generations would be even more likely to produce and be social.

Since it is easy to be the most productive chicken when you have pecked all the others to death, it's no surprise that the super chicken was also a nasty little bugger with no friends.

Hearing this you might say, "Those super chickens sound a lot like the people I work with." And that shouldn't surprise us. Business professionals and professional athletes have been selected and groomed for success just like the Dekalb XL chicken.

From a young age, athletes join their local leagues and are trained to win. If they are good, they earn a spot on a children's traveling team competing against the best in the area. If that goes well, and their stats are strong enough, they can be selected for a prestigious high school program, earn all-American status, or even be part of

Team USA and possibly go to the Olympics. At each stage, if they compete well enough and stand out among their peers they are rewarded. Standing out in high school means they will get scouted by college programs. Then you are in the big leagues. As a student-athlete you can make a fortune, but that's only the start. If you do well in college sports, it means potentially being drafted into a professional league. Your entire career has been one challenge after another to prove you are better than everyone around you so you can get to the next level. You are a super chicken fighting for stats, attention, and rewards. In a system like this, even when you are on the same team as someone, they are still your enemy competing for the same awards and limited positions on the all-star teams, endorsement contracts, and media coverage. At a certain point, the only way to keep standing out is by making sure others don't get attention. They are super chickens pecking at each other.

Maybe you didn't have the competitive sports experience, but you've probably seen the same situation in the business world. As children, we are taught that we have to do well in grade school, so we can go to a prestigious high school. Then if we compete hard enough, get great grades, and score high enough on the tests, we can go to a top college. Here is where things get more intense. You are now with a much more impressive group of people, competing for top marks, internships, and eventually a plum job. Once we are at the company, our coworkers, the people we are supposed to be collaborating with to succeed, are also our competition for promotion and status markers like bonuses. The further you go through the processes, the bigger the rewards and incentives, and when only one person can hold that coveted C-suite position, it means it is either you or them. Corporate America has made us think that the only way to succeed is through competition, but when we compete against our collaborators, we turn into super chickens. The only way we win is by everyone else losing. And if I have to make sure everyone else loses/gets pecked to death, there is no way the team can succeed.

So, when sports teams select for pure talent, they don't get super teams; they get self-centered personalities, and super-chicken-style competition. Does this remind you of how Team USA basketball consistently beat the NBA All-Stars back in 1980? The NBA All-Stars had so much talent that they weren't just competing against the other team; they were competing with each other for minutes of play and who would take the shot. The only statistic in basketball that correlates to salary and social media following is points scored. Not shooting percentage, rebounds, or anything else people measure. This means that a player's main incentive is to shoot the ball. Even if their teammates might be in a better position to score, they will take the worst shot because if it does go in, it does them well.

Meanwhile, the Team USA student-athletes trained together for a singular goal: to represent the US. They were a super team going up against the biggest super chickens in basketball, and although one-on-one they probably never would have stood a chance, as a team they could maximize their intelligence. Remember the passing metric I shared with you in the last chapter? Passing demonstrates that a player is shifting focus from themselves to the team. It means they are willing to give up taking the shot so that someone else in a better position can score. An effective coach takes talented people who have been raised as super chickens and bred to compete with each other, and gets them to pass more, share resources, and support each other. That's what great leaders do too. When we focus too much on an individual leader or an individual superstar, we can forget that teams win, not individuals.

Which Cult Are You In?

We see the same trend in our careers. People have progressively become more focused on their personal brand, social media following, perfectly curated LinkedIn profile, and that ridiculous podcast they record that no one wants to hear. We have entered a moment where people have fallen into what I call the "cult of self," where their focus is their own desires at the exclusion or cost of everyone else's. This may sound narcissistic or egotistical, but it is a natural response considering recent history.

There was a time when people would work at the same company for decades. Through the 1970s, major American companies had a "retain and reinvest" model where they would hire people and try to keep and develop them over decades. Unfortunately, when the global recession hit in 1980, companies had too many employees and needed to do the unthinkable: let some of them go. Once the trend was set, companies continued the habit. The 1990s brought in shareholder activists; these were investors with a lot of stock in the company, who used it to put pressure on management to force a result—specifically, actions the investors hoped would make the stock more valuable. So now we find ourselves in a situation where companies will do massive layoffs to ensure their stock value stays high, but employees have no sense of security or stability. Talk about a lack of benevolence.

If I can be a hardworking, productive, and effective employee, and the company might get rid of me at any moment to please shareholders, then part of my work time will switch from being focused on the company to focusing on myself. That "me" time will be used to develop my brand, my resume, my social media presence, and my connections so I have my next job lined up. Companies have incentivized us to hedge our bets, by putting less effort into work and more attention into finding "side hustles" so we don't go hungry if the job disappears. Meanwhile, social media rewards oversharing, influence-making, and a watered-down notion of "engagement"; the more we focus on ourselves, the larger the following we have, the more money we make, and the better our lives become. Or at least that's the argument. But remember, in the super chicken experiment, the super team laid more eggs and were healthier than the super chickens; in basketball, teams that collaborated more outdid those who were selfish; and in business, teams with higher levels of psychological safety outperformed. Any gains from the cult of self may come at the cost of satisfaction, connection, belonging, and lasting achievement—the very things that separate us from the super chickens.

You may have noticed that humans aren't particularly fast or strong compared to many other animals, like the cheetah. Instead, our species has survived because of group effort. Cheetahs, on the other hand, are famous for having no friends. If you have ever had a night out with a cheetah, you know they go way too hard way too fast and then sleep the rest of the day. That's no fun.

If we go back forty thousand years, there is almost no chance a mother caring for a newborn could survive without the support of a community. She would have to hunt and gather while feeding, caring for, and protecting a child. Humans have survived because we evolved to work together, and not only were we wired for this, but when we are isolated, we tend to become depressed and die younger. Like it or not, we need each other, and we are at our best when we are together.

A lot has changed in the past few years, and some of those changes have really sucked. What do you think happens when you take a society that's already trending toward self-obsession and send it home to work for a few years because of a global pandemic? Do you think they will suddenly become group-oriented, or do you think the unexpected isolation and lack of exposure to the organization will make them even more self-obsessed? (The author asked rhetorically.) Not surprisingly, we've fallen even deeper into the cult of self. When we aren't exposed to other people, then we don't think about their challenges, interests, or concerns, and we just spend more time thinking about ourselves.

It's tempting to think that if focusing on ourselves leads to less overall success, less happiness, and less satisfaction, then we are better off at the other extreme: let's make it all about the team! What if we were to focus only on the group, eliminating our egos completely?

If the problem with the cult of self is that optimizing for the individual makes the group less effective and the team members less engaged and satisfied, then the problem with a team-only, cultish approach is that it undervalues individual differences, identities, and talents, and suppresses divergent thinking and constructive conflict. If history tells us anything (Heaven's Gate, Branch Davidians, NXIVM, etc.), this doesn't go well, because whatever the cult leader says becomes the truth, and if you raise a question or try to challenge something you will be shamed or punished. Chances are, in the workplace, the bigger risk would be groupthink. The idea was defined by Yale University research psychologist Irving Janis to describe how terrible decisions are made by a group where the members value harmony and conformity more than realistically evaluating alternate options. When we lack an appreciation for individuality and different perspectives, we can't see the errors in our thinking or other options, and we tend to increase team stupidity and make terrible choices like the Iraq War, or wearing all denim, or basically anything else humanity did in 2003. Just ask my roommates back then; my bad choices didn't stop at parachute pants.

Remember my nerdy digression about the work culture on the Death Star? Right, so we obviously don't want that. There needs to be a middle ground where people:

1. Are willing to give up status and rewards to achieve team objectives.

2. Have a voice and are safe to express it.

You might be thinking, Jon, this sounds lovely, but I don't have time for six generations of super-chicken breeding to create the perfect team. I've got quarterly KPIs to meet right now. So how do I find people who embody these values or get my team to act like this?

Frankly, this is a really tough question, and to start to find an answer, we need to unravel a mystery.

Getting the Team to Stick Together

If you are building a championship basketball team, we have already learned that too much talent can be a problem. But the solution shouldn't be to team up a bunch of stars with fifth graders. An incompetent teammate can do more damage than a superstar can improve the situation. So how do we find the right balance of team members, and how do we put those people together? The answer may hide in a unique approach to basketball.

By the end of the 2005–06 NBA season, the Houston Rockets needed a change. They had a record of 34 wins and a massive 48 losses. To turn the team around, the owner brought in Daryl Morey, who would eventually become their general manager. In basketball, teams have a salary cap that they can spend in any way they want, but most of the Rockets' budget was locked in for the next few years with two star players, Yao Ming and Tracy McGrady. Without much budget to play with, Morey had to get creative.

So why is it that when Morey made a short list of players he wanted most, near the top was Shane Battier, someone Morey described as "at best, a marginal NBA athlete," who "can't dribble, he's slow and hasn't got much body control"? In fact, every statistic was disappointing. He didn't score often, didn't block shots, steal, or get many rebounds or assists. Frankly, he sounds like me but taller and better-looking. Anyone looking at traditional stats would say it would be a mistake to add this person to an already losing team. But Morey understood something that was made famous by academic Aaron Levenstein: "Statistics are like bikinis. What they reveal is suggestive, but what they conceal is vital."

The traditional NBA stats might tell you "suggestive" info, like how many points a player has at the end of the game. In business, work stats might highlight how much a salesperson sold, or if an employee came into the office a certain number of days a quarter, but they "conceal" the context. Did the player score by taking a lot of bad shots costing the team more wins? Is the salesperson being mentored by someone who should be the sales manager? Is the employee out of the office because they are on-site with customers every day? NBA stats don't tell you how the players interact or if those shots went in because someone else was strategic enough to block an opponent. Meanwhile, corporate stats like hours logged into a system, number of emails sent, and days in the office don't help us understand if these dynamics lead to success or if people are wasting time doing busywork.

Since Morey didn't have the money for more superstars, he needed to find anomalies: players who were undervalued and underutilized. He had to look past the traditional information and interpretations. One piece of information about Battier that stood out to Morey was what is known as a plus-minus.

The plus-minus tells us how much more the team scores when a player is on the court. You expect that if you add LeBron James to your team, it adds several points to your team's total (a plus), but if you add me at 5'10" with my scrawny legs, no ability to jump, and constant lower back pain, you expect the other team to score a lot more (a minus). Admittedly, this stat can be misleading. If a bad player is always teamed up with great players, then it could look like their plus-minus is high. So, Morey and his team found a way to account for this, and what they discovered was that Battier was one of the most undervalued players in the NBA.

As Morey explained in an interview with Michael Lewis, a star player might have a plus-minus of 14 at their peak. At Battier's peak, he was close to 10, and over the course of his career, he was a plus 6. Morey points out, "Plus six is enormous.... It's the difference between forty-one wins and sixty wins." So how could Shane Battier have such a huge plus-minus but no clear meaningful impact? The answer is that statistics are indeed like bikinis, and what the traditional numbers hide is that Shane is a glue player.

It helps to understand Shane's background. Growing up in Birmingham, Michigan, Battier did not fit in. The neighborhood was almost exclusively white, and in the early 1980s people saw him as something else. His father was the only black man in town, and his mother was white, so Shane is "mixed." That is much more common these days but back then it was tough for a kid.

In Shane's words, "This was the early eighties, mind you. There were no mixed brothers on [TV shows like] *The A-Team* or *Three's Company*." People had no cultural reference in seeing someone who looked like him; it was clear he didn't fit. But Shane was a smart kid, and he realized that "people like people who help them win. It doesn't matter if someone thinks you're goofy or nerdy or different, if you can help someone win at something, they'll like you." Shane began a lifelong journey into being the best teammate anyone could have. It started on the kickball field, diving for balls, sliding headfirst whenever he could—and winning. You can see Shane's super skills forming from a young age. And because of these super skills, people would feel they would have a better future. They liked having Shane on their team because it meant they could win.

I don't know your experience growing up, but when I was in grade school, we had a few athletic kids in the class, and they always had an ego about being better than the rest of us. They would trash-talk and make fun of us uncoordinated kids. Shane was different. While some people rise up by pushing others down, like those super chickens, Shane did the opposite: he would turn a team into a super team. As Shane explained, "It was never about the credit that I received. It was about the credit the team got." He wasn't trying to feed his ego; he was trying to find a way for everyone to win and connect in the process. That was his super skill.

Shane is a glue player, someone who may not have any specific technical skill that stands out at the superstar level but is so good with group dynamics, bonding, building trust, and elevating everyone's game that the team outperforms because of his participation. Glue players might not be the stars that shine the brightest, but their gravity is so strong that they pull everyone else into a tight orbit, performing at their best.

Shane would eventually move on from the kickball diamond to

the basketball court and enroll at Duke University, where he played for the Blue Devils. At 6'8" and 220 pounds, his tenacity and team orientation gave him a reputation as an exceptional athlete. As a part of the Blue Devils 2001 NCAA national championship team, he was named the national player of the year for US men's college basketball.

Still, it's one thing to be a great student-athlete, and something completely different to play in the NBA. As the talent level went up around Battier, it was harder to see the real impact he was having. When the stats focus on individual contributions, you miss everything that makes a great team. Remember, the too-much-talent problem happens when you have high task interdependence, like you do in basketball. As you add super chickens and measure them solely on individual stats, you shift the focus away from what makes a team win to what will make individual stars look good. The NBA's stats are focused on continuing to develop super chickens rather than super teams.

The same is true for business teams. When you look at how recognition and rewards are distributed at corporations, they encourage super-chicken behavior rather than super teams. They focus on metrics that are easy to measure (total sales, days in office, hours worked) rather than contributions that are harder to see, such as impact on team performance, increase in coworker retention, ability to work with difficult talent, ability to translate technical ideas to others, etc. Unfortunately, these traditional metrics all give status and compensation to super chickens, and so the organization never considers the people who don't have time or interest to compete because they are too busy making sure the team works. In traditional family structures, we call these underappreciated super people "Mom."

Somehow Morey was able to see past the traditional stats and spot what no one else did, and brought Battier on the team. Morey would call him "Lego," because when Battier was on the court, all the pieces fit together, and everyone could do their jobs better. In the interview with Michael Lewis, Battier was described as "the most abnormally unselfish basketball player [Morey] has ever seen. Or rather, the player who seems one step ahead of the analysts, helping the team in all sorts of subtle, hard-to-measure ways that appear to violate his own personal interests."

What are some of these hard-to-measure behaviors, habits, skills, and experiences?

- One of his coaches would complain that he didn't take enough shots. While most players take too many and don't pass enough, Battier knew his teammate's stats and knew whom to pass the ball to and when so that the odds were in their favor.

- He once asked his coach to bench him during a game and give him fewer playtime minutes so he could come out every time the opponent's best shooter was on the court and have the energy to defend him.

- He would memorize the stats of the opposing team, knowing where each player did their best and worst, so that while defending them he could force them into their weakest locations.

- Battier talked to his teammates a lot more than anyone else on the court; he would watch how the game unfolded, how the opposing team played, and would constantly communicate important information.

- Battier memorized the names of each of his opponent's kindergarten teachers, so when they missed a shot, he would whisper, "Mrs. Clark would be disappointed in you," which psychologically destroyed his opponent. Right, so obviously I can't prove that the last one ever happened. But you can't prove it didn't either!

You can begin to see how fundamentally different his attitude was and how much it contributed to the Rockets going from a losing record of only 34 wins the season before he joined to a winning record in the 50s for the next three seasons once he was part of the team.

During the 2008 Olympic Games, three Team USA basketball players—LeBron James, Dwyane Wade, and Chris Bosh—became close friends and hatched a plan to play on the same team and dominate the NBA. In 2010 they all landed on the Miami Heat. When asked about how many championships they would win together, LeBron famously said, "Not two, not three, not four, not five, not six, not seven . . . and when I say that I really believe it." During their first season LeBron began referring to themselves as "the Heatles," comparing themselves to the Beatles, the greatest music group in history, and their ability to sell out stadiums as they toured. But he may have gotten a little ahead of himself. Although they had a fantastic record, at the end of their first season together they didn't take home a championship.

Even with all the talent of the "Big Three," as they became known, it wasn't enough. It's natural that when an organization is busy focused on the super chickens, they miss what's going on with the rest of the team, or the little twelve, as they jokingly referred to themselves. Something changed in 2011, because for the next two years, they won back-to-back championships. It just seemed everything fit better, and things were clicking like LEGO pieces. Wait, does that sound like someone we know? Cue the entry music because Shane Battier made an appearance. Yes, that's right, if you looked at the roster you would surely notice the human Elmer's bottle, Shane Battier, doing what he does best: bringing the team together and not making a fuss of it.

Can we say that Shane was the reason the Miami Heat won those championships? Of course not, and even suggesting something like that misses the point. We love to say it was one person who saved the day. It is an easy and fun story, but it keeps us in the world of super chickens. Teams win because of everyone's contributions; they are complex systems, and competition is unpredictable. But what I am suggesting is that Battier's unique super skills added to the team dynamics to move them from a group of super chickens closer to a super team. Most people would never notice, because we tend to measure what is easy to see and not what is useful.

After back-to-back championships, the Heat were on fire. They were well on their way to an unstoppable dynasty. But even with all their talent, when they made it to the NBA Finals in 2014 they lost, 4 games to 1, against the San Antonio Spurs. The Spurs' coach, Gregg Popovich, or Pop as people call him, is so legendary at creating trusted teams that he is referred to as "Impossible," having won five NBA championships over his career and never having the super talent of the Heatles. When statistician Neil Paine did an analysis on how many wins NBA coaches should have based on the talent on their roster, he saw that every coach had just about the expected number of game wins, except for one: good ol' Pop. He won an outlandish 117 games more than he should have. Why? Because Popovich, much like Shane Battier, is a glue player.

When in an interview after a game LeBron was asked about the Spurs, he said, "That's team basketball and that's how team basketball should be played. . . . It's selfless. Guys move, cut, pass, you've got a shot, you take it. But it's all for the team and it's never about the individual. That's the brand of basketball, and that's how team basketball should be played."

After that season the Heatles broke up, and no, it wasn't Yoko Ono who caused it; it was of course self-interest. When the Heat's head coach, Pat Riley, asked LeBron to make a personal sacrifice and take a pay cut, to use some budget to improve the team, LeBron went back to the Cleveland Cavaliers for more pay. Frankly, who could blame him. Still, it was the end of an era and after thirteen years on NBA courts, Battier chose to retire and focus on bringing his unique gifts to the way companies operate. As of this writing he sits on four corporate boards.

So now we may have our answer to the question that we started with: How do we get teams to operate at their best? We learned that if we truly want our teams to succeed, we have to escape the way we think about and reward talent; instead of breeding super chickens like the DeKalb XL that pecks their teammates to death, we want to create super teams. William Muir did that by breeding his chickens, generation after generation, and rewarding the behavior that he wanted. In the corporate world that looks like creating a culture where people are rewarded and get status for healthy team behaviors.

The second thing we need to do is start looking at the harder-to-see, more meaningful stats, those that show us when people are contributing significant value to the team's success, like glue players do. We also need to get rid of those that are toxic.

In the next three chapters we will tackle the specific steps to apply these strategies, and the incredible new scientific research that unlocks your team's intelligence. So, you can create a team you are both proud to be a part of and enjoy working with.

Ideas in Action

- Too much focus on recruiting and retaining star talent creates the too-much-talent problem. On teams where people's work depends on each other (high task interdependence), having more than 50–60 percent top talent actually reduces success.

- Cultural changes over the last several decades have caused people to focus more on themselves and less on the company or organization. In work with high task interdependence, maximizing personal results will come at the cost of the team's success.

- A healthy balance is required for team success, where team members are willing to give up personal status and rewards to achieve team objectives, but still have a voice and are safe to express it.

- To increase team intelligence, here are two approaches:
  - Muir succeeded in breeding KGB (kinder, gentler birds) that lay more eggs as a team than the Dekalb XL super chickens could as a group. He did this by rewarding both results and prosocial behavior. The super chickens were only rewarded for results, so they produced them at the cost of team success.
  - Daryl Morey took the other approach: he looked past the obvious stats and searched for what was useful. He found that there are players who are undervalued, like Shane Battier, yet create a huge impact on team results but are often overlooked. As

a result, he was able to build a team with the skills he needed.

- Glue players like Shane Battier have an ability to bring a team together and have them function more like a super team, and less like super chickens.

Chapter 6

Team Intelligence—Reasoning

Have you ever met someone and thought to yourself, *Wow, that person is really smart*? What do we mean by that? I think I first noticed in grade school that some people weren't just good in one class; they were great at all of them. As someone who grew up with dyslexia, I struggled in so many classes that I was in awe of these kids. Researchers would say that those people have high "general intelligence," meaning they are good at reasoning in a lot of areas. That made me wonder, is there a general intelligence for teams? Are there teams that are great at tackling almost any challenge, from managing a complex long-term project to crushing the escape room at the company outing?

In the last few chapters, we realized that talent alone isn't the answer, and in fact can be detrimental. Effective teams succeed because they are connected and build trust, but that is just a first step. Muir taught us that we can created a super team, free of super chickens, by rewarding the right behavior. Meanwhile, Morey looked past traditional metrics and discovered glue players. People who embody traits that cause teams and even super chicken teammates to outperform. Now we need to ask what we should focus on. What are the habits that cause a team to perform at its best? What do we need to reinforce and reward, or what characteristics do we need to find in the people we work with or hire?

The answer can be found in the research of Anita Williams Woolley from Carnegie Mellon University. For more than twenty years

Woolley has been obsessed with the question of how to get teams to operate smarter, to exceed the sum of their parts.

Woolley began by inviting people into her lab and testing their IQ along with a few other characteristics. She then put them in teams and gave them a series of tasks to complete, ranging from pattern recognition puzzles and creative use activities (for example, listing all possible uses of a brick) to developing a strategy for how to best use a car for a shared shopping trip (not easy when considering priorities, item availability, best routes, and store locations). She and her colleagues wanted to see how quickly and effectively the teams could solve the problems. Which ones consistently made the best use of the resources they were given, as quickly as possible? In these situations, somehow the teams were more effective together.

What she discovered was that the intelligence of the group had nothing to do with the average of their IQs or the IQ of the smartest person. In other words, adding a genius like Einstein to a group won't necessarily make the team any smarter or more effective, though it will up their mustache game (which is not nothing). Woolley and her colleagues found no relationship between how much team members liked each other (a measure of team cohesion) or how motivated they were to solve the problems thrown at them. You would think that competitive teams would push to get things done faster and better, but none of these things made a difference. So, what did?

It turns out that groups quickly develop patterns for working together, and these habits and behaviors define their team intelligence. It didn't matter if a group did one task in the lab or ten of them: the patterns were the same. If they were good at one, they were good at all of them. This is incredibly convenient for us since it means that we can evaluate our own team intelligence once we understand what these habits are, and which ones make the team smarter or stupider.

They break down into three areas:

- *Reasoning:* How they get to the solution with the resources they have

- *Attention:* How they focus, on what, and when

- *Resources:* How they access the knowledge, and experience of the team members

Let's delve into an example that dramatically highlights how this first pillar—reasoning—plays out in the real world. In subsequent chapters, we'll dive deeper into the other two: attention and resources.

E Pluribus Unum

Tucked away in Maricopa County, Arizona, sits a training facility for one of the most elite teams of pilots in the world. Thanks to movies like *Top Gun* and its sequel, when we imagine the best pilots in the world, we expect people with absolute confidence and an air of superiority who push the limits of their bodies to accomplish tactical maneuvers that seem to defy the laws of physics. If anyone has earned the right to be arrogant super chickens, it would be the incredible pilots of the F-35 fighter jets. These fifth-generation single-pilot planes are the most advanced fighting machines in the world. At a staggering cost of about $100 million per plane, $50 million to train a barely competent pilot, and up to $50,000 to fly for an hour, if I were a pilot of one of these planes, I would absolutely feel cooler and better than everyone else (except for you; you are way cooler than me, which is why you are giving this book a five-star rating). Rumor has it that as few as one out of every thousand people who apply for pilot training will have the privilege of flying the F-35. One of these pilots is Lieutenant Colonel Justin "Hasard" Lee, who after flying more than eighty F-16 combat missions in Afghanistan was handpicked for the F-35 program.

As Hasard explains, in the 1970s and '80s, fighter jet warfare was more like *Top Gun*. The cream of the crop would participate in one-on-one air combat known as dogfighting (what we would call super chicken fighting). It was an activity where being the best meant that you survived. Today, much like the complexities of running a business, warfare has evolved. To fly a single mission involving the F-35, Hasard may need to convene hundreds of people in the briefing. Yes, hundreds.

When I heard this, it sounded like some excessive joke about military waste, until Hasard explained who may be in the briefing and why. You might have military intelligence come with satellite data about the enemy's resources, a cyber team that can hack their systems, a space force that can jam signals using satellites. The CIA might bring additional intel, not to mention support planes, helicopters, and ground troops, to name a few. If you have to go in and save a downed pilot, bomb an enemy bunker, or back up troops on the ground, you need support from countless people.

The challenge with any group is to make sure that you can plan the best route from where you are to your goal. We call this the ability to reason. The more people we add to a team, the more skills, perspectives, and resources, but also more conflict. For a pilot like Hasard, no matter how extraordinary and special he is, he can't afford to be the arrogant, pompous, self-centered jerk we see in the movies; those days are over. Instead of telling people what to do, his job is to develop consensus among the group and make sure everyone is clear on the plan, because if they fail, the lives and safety of his fellow servicepeople will be at stake.

You might think that, well, this is the military; people have their orders, and soldiers just follow the chain of command. But never underestimate conflicting goals within an organization. A basketball team may want to win, but each of the players also wants to be the person who scores the winning shot. Their organizational, team, and personal goals don't always align. During his time in Afghanistan, Hasard flew eighty-two combat missions, but often there was tension between international priorities, the Air Force wanting to go after high-value targets by maybe bombing a building, the Army wanting him to back up troops, and Italian forces needing additional support. This is why if you want to unlock a team's ability to reason, you need alignment. We need to make sure that the whole team is heading toward the same North Star. In other words, it is impossible to travel together if one of us is taking a midnight train to Georgia and the other has a ticket for the long way around (two bottles of whiskey for the way).

The same issue exists in some professional sports teams and rears its head in the corporate world. One study found that more than 60 percent of employees don't know their company's mission statement, and of the few who did, almost 60 percent of them found it unmotivating. Imagine going on a hike with 100 people, where 60 have no idea where the group is going and so they are wandering aimlessly and have to be constantly brought back to the trail; the other 40 people do have a map, but 24 of them don't really care about whether or not they follow it and would rather lie in a meadow and pick dandelions. Think about how much time is wasted when only 16 people both know the mission and are motivated to achieve it. Now consider how much worse it is when one of these 100 people is trying to convince some of the people to go in an entirely different direction—say, to the park to play pickleball. One study estimates that the negative impact of this lack of alignment costs companies between $450 billion and $550 billion a year.

One company that understands the importance of alignment is Microsoft. On every ID badge, it says, "Our mission is to empower every person and every organization on the planet to achieve more." But let's be honest: most large companies aren't as clear as Microsoft, and frankly, if you have thousands of products in different categories, it can be hard to distill that mission as well as they did. But there is no excuse for an individual team not to know its objectives. This clarity is something you should be able to achieve no matter what your role is on the team.

To solve for the alignment issue, the military established what they call "commander's intent." Usually a general or admiral who is in charge of the region defines what a successful overall outcome will look like at the end. Then it is the commander's responsibility to make sure their missions align to that goal. Every person involved in a mission has to know what the commander's intent and the mission goal is, before planning begins, so that they can reason a solution. But for Hasard it's not enough that people know the goal; he needs a greater alignment at each level.

1. *Commander's intent:* Everyone in the organization needs to know the broader goal.

2. *Mission parameters:* What is the end state of this mission?

3. *Team objectives:* Each team needs to be clear on what they contribute to fulfilling the mission and why.

4. *Contributions to the team:* Team members are clear on how their role supports the team and the overall mission.

5. *Personal goals:* The person's direct commander should ensure that fulfilling what matters to the person aligns with all the other objectives.

At the office, if someone's personal goals don't align with the team or organization, they will be working against the group. They might want to get a promotion, a raise, speak at a meeting, move cities, or even just make a joke in the team group chat that earns double-digit laugh emojis. By aligning personal, team, and company goals like a total eclipse of corporate synergy, you can make sure everyone is working in the same direction.

So, when Hasard convenes several hundred people for a mission briefing, his first objective is to unlock team intelligence and create alignment. He needs everyone to understand the commander's intent, team roles, and individual roles, and why they need to accomplish the mission.

You might ask why I keep emphasizing that people should understand not just the goal but the reason for it. Any soldier will tell you, no plan survives first contact with the enemy. With the fog and friction of war, you come up against unexpected challenges, injuries, dangers, and opposition, and the original strategy might not work anymore. That's why intention comes before tactics.

During the peak of the Cold War with the Soviet Union, there was a lot of debate about how pilots should be trained. The Soviets preferred pilots who were technically capable but depended on communication with commanders on the ground, getting new orders based on changing conditions. This would allow pilots to focus all their effort on action, rather than decision-making. Think of it more like a remote-control pilot. Meanwhile, the US took the approach that the pilots have to be the final decision-makers. The moment they are leading a mission, they are the ones on the front lines with the most information, so they should be in charge. This means that the pilots needed to be trained to make fast and accurate decisions while they were potentially being fired on or in a dogfight. If you remember the story of Terry Virts almost flying into a mountain, it's clearly a challenge to manage everything.

Over time, the answer became clear. Although the Soviet pilots had incredible technical skills, they didn't have the ability to handle the constantly changing conditions of real combat. When every decision needs to go through a superior, it deadlocks the team members from handling the problem in front of them. This is why it is so important for people to understand where we are going, why we chose this path, and what their role is, because when the situation inevitably changes, then the people on the ground understand why those goals are or aren't important anymore, and if they need to, they can come up with an alternate plan to accomplish them.

You can see that a lack of alignment can destroy any team's ability to reason. In fact, if you want to make a team significantly more stupid, it is really easy: either reward people for going in opposite directions, or have people fight for control; it will split the team.

Who's in Charge?

One of the most interesting insights gleaned from Woolley's research is that the smartest teams don't necessarily need a formal leader. Different people lead at different times based on their expertise. In this way, the team learns to deploy its resources optimally, depending on the task at hand.

The fastest way to destroy intelligence is by having people fight to be the leader. You have probably noticed that when there are internal struggles for power, the team loses its ability to get work done and looks really dumb. It is a classic super chicken scenario. Not only does it split the team's alignment, but the people fighting for control aren't working; they are wasting time politicking, which doesn't just look dumb, but is objectively quite stupid. Power struggles can be incredibly destructive, and for relatively meaningless tasks, it may just not be worth the battle. Thus the saying "Pick your battles" is particularly important when it comes to preserving and nurturing a team's intelligence. Sometimes having a team leader is necessary—like when the fate of the company or a product's launch is at stake. Other times it's just petty politics. Move on!

But for those times and those teams who do have a leader, it should come as no surprise, based on everything I have shared so far, that the most effective team leaders aren't looking to dominate the group. The research confirms that teams that were overly managed by one person became stupider, like those cults we learned about, or your family on vacation when Dad refused to ask for directions. When a single leader dominates the group, it minimizes what the rest of the team can contribute—it diminishes the team's resources.

In sports, you sometimes see this. When a star player is injured, the rest of the team can have the space to contribute and shine. You may have experienced this at work too. When your boss was away, people stepped up, and the team became more intelligent.

Does this mean that companies led by dominant personalities don't succeed? Of course they can, but they don't necessarily unlock the most talent and value from people. Frankly, when leaders are overly dominant, it destroys trust and belonging, so they tend to have a hard time recruiting and keeping talent.

Woolley and her team were able to simulate what happens when you bring together expert talent that is disconnected to tackle a problem, by inviting strangers into her lab to solve terrorism scenarios. They created two types of teams: Generalists, people who knew nothing about terrorism, and teams of Subject Matter Experts. The results were shocking and, if you work in intelligence, pretty embarrassing. The Generalists straight out beat the Subject Matter Experts in the greatest upset since the 1980s NBA All-Stars losing to a bunch of college kids (and with even higher geopolitical stakes!).

Next, the researchers put each team through a communication activity to help them build trust and connect more effectively. Then they repeated the experiment. This time the Subject Matter Experts demolished the Generalists; it wasn't even close.

What made the difference? The newfound connection and trust that had been developed among team members. Once again, we see how right Dwight D. Eisenhower was about the value of connection. Making the effort to connect the team, the way he connected the US with highways, might take a lot of time at the beginning but it allows for everything to work better and for faster results moving forward. It is also why glue players are so important; it is in their nature to grow those connections within the team.

The ability to reason is just the first of three pillars of team intelligence; to truly unlock your group's collective genius, we still need to understand attention and resources. So let's dive in and learn about how the toy of the century almost went bankrupt.

Ideas in Action

So, what do we do with our new understanding of reasoning, the first pillar of team intelligence?

The good news is that the ingredients of team intelligence are things you can control, nurture, and build through alignment, connection, and trust.

As the leader you can:

- *Create clarity:* Make sure the team's objectives are clear, and that each person understands the commander's intent, what success looks like when the mission is accomplished, and how their work contributes to that mission.

- *Repeat objectives often:* You will know you have done a good job when team members start quoting you or making fun of the fact that you are always talking about the goal.

- *Assign an alignment person:* In every meeting, it is their job to make sure there is clarity on where the team is going, the roles for each team member, and the next steps.

- *Create full alignment:* Connect the team goals to people's personal goals. For example, you might say:
    - I know you have been wanting to present more, so I am assigning you to write the deck for next week's presentation. It will help you practice your

storytelling and will build up your confidence for when you do your first pitch.
- I plan on submitting your name for promotion, and I would love to include this project to justify it, so it needs to be perfectly buttoned up. Can you go through it carefully before we submit it, so that both the client can be happy and you look great internally?

- *Celebrate alignment:* Publicly and privately compliment the person who is brave enough to make sure everyone is on the same page. We want to give status to the skill, so people value it more and understand its importance.

- *Celebrate the team:* When the team succeeds, it's tempting to celebrate the outgoing extrovert. Instead, celebrate everyone, and make sure to acknowledge all the work that you know happened and all the work that you will never know happened because people took care of problems before they were brought to you or came up in a meeting. Thank and acknowledge everyone. Use this as a reason to do activities that further increase team trust.

- *Give group bonuses:* This may not be in your control, but, if possible, avoid individual bonuses for work that is group-oriented. It gives conflicting signals.

- *Reinforce personal goals:* Highlight when accomplishing team goals fulfills or leads to accomplishing personal goals.

- *Reinforce leadership fluidity:* Compliment the team when you see them passing the leadership baton around, and don't be afraid to intervene when you see teams being split by leadership conflicts.

- *Dance:* Kevin Bacon fought for our right to dance, so let's repay his sacrifice by engaging in some fun, morale-boosting moving and shaking.

Even if you aren't the leader, or the group doesn't have a formal leader, you can help your team develop a greater team intelligence. Ask lots of questions, such as:

- I can see how [Person 1]'s work will contribute to our goal of [Insert Goal] but would my work conflict with this, or am I overthinking things?

- I just want to make sure that our team's goal is still [Insert Goal], or did things change because of [e.g., new management, economic shifts, someone left the team, etc.]?

- If we allocate budget to [Insert Project], will it leave enough for our goal of [Insert Goal]?

Asking questions like this not only reinforces the team's sense of a shared mission, but it also helps them test and realign their reasoning, problem-solving, and decision-making skills around those goals.

Chapter 7
Team Intelligence—Attention

In the early 2000s, LEGO, the Danish company synonymous with parents screaming when they accidentally step on a little plastic brick, was in trouble. From the outside, it looked like an example of how to take a fifty-plus-year-old brand and keep it relevant to a young audience. It was an innovation factory. In fact, by 1999, when *Fortune* magazine crowned it the toy of the twentieth century, they wrote that "slightly more than 203 billion have been made. It seems safe to assume that at least ten billion are under sofa cushions, three billion are inside vacuum cleaners, and right now a barefoot parent has just stepped on one." LEGO was the envy of the toy industry.

But in the early 1990s, when sales began to slump and they feared that all kids wanted was videogames, LEGO started to release a never-ending collection of new products. By 2003 they had tripled the number of products they made. This was combined with an innovation kick that launched LEGO electronics, jewelry, theme parks, education centers, and now-famous partnerships with entertainment franchises like Star Wars and Harry Potter. It was doing everything a modern company was supposed to; it hired a diverse group of innovative thinkers who were creating new markets for the company to expand its reach. They applied the most effective approaches to product development and feedback, but they were at risk of going under.

In 2003 the company lost a staggering $300 million and by 2004 it was projected to lose $400 million. They were running out of cash and were about to go bankrupt. All those new products didn't actually increase sales; they just made production more expensive, and the partnerships with Harry Potter and Star Wars were great but only when a movie came out to promote it.

You might think this was a company that wasn't clear on its goal; it lacked a North Star, so it got lost. But they knew their mission: LEGO was to become "the world's strongest brand among families by 2005." The ethos of LEGO was clear to everyone; in fact, the name comes from the Danish phrase "leg godt," which means to play well. Everyone at LEGO was serious about play and achieving the ultimate status among families.

So, what was going on at the company? It had corporate attention-deficit disorder. When LEGO first started it was a wooden toy company, but at one point their leadership realized that the true potential was incredibly high-quality interlocking bricks. By standardizing the brick as the centerpiece of the company, kids would be able to buy set after set and expand a universe that fulfills their imagination. Once a child had a set for a house, they could add sets and turn it into a town, or add a space station or a pirate ship, but it all worked together. In hopes of breaking their slump, they lost sight of what makes the company special. It had expanded so fast into every possible industry that they forgot what they do best and what they needed to focus on.

This won't surprise you, but if you want to make a team stupider, spread its attention and constantly distract it. You know this. Any time you are trying to get work done, and you begin to get notification after notification, and then someone calls you or stops by your office for a question or a file, you can't get anything done. People need a certain amount of time to get focused on their work, and every interruption resets that. When we are distracted, either we don't get work done, or if we do it is not great quality. We and our teams get stupider.

Here we have our answer: LEGO's corporate ADD was out of control. According to David C. Robertson, the author of *Brick by Brick*, the company launched 140 LEGO education centers in South Korea to teach kids through play. Their young children's line of Duplo bricks, which was the second-most-popular toy in Europe, was replaced with LEGO Explorer, brickless games that looked like Fisher Price toys. The team members who raised concerns were silenced and were told to be supportive or leave. The company even released non-LEGO-based assembly kits and action figures, which were incredibly unpopular and quickly discontinued. For some unknown reason, after launching a series of money-losing LEGO stores, they wanted to expand them to 300 locations. If all this wasn't enough, they went from producing about 6,000 LEGO pieces to over 14,000 and from six colors to over fifty, making manufacturing insanely complex and expensive.

Although people could argue this was innovation, none of these things made the company better or more successful. It was all a distraction. For them to unlock the collective genius of the organization and increase their team intelligence, they needed to manage their attention.

So, in October 2004, Jørgen Vig Knudstorp was appointed as CEO of LEGO to turn the company around. As a thirty-five-year-old former consultant, he may have struck people as a surprising choice, but what the leadership needed was exactly what he brought: analytical skills and a deep understanding of business operations. Up until then, they were on a spending spree like children with their parents' credit cards. He had to be the adult in the room.

His strategy was simple. For the company to "pull back from the abyss, [they] . . . would have to value discipline and focus, as much as creativity." The company would put all its attention on its core products and ensure that they were profitable. Everyone wanted a big innovative strategy that would fix everything, but Knudstorp refused to give them one. They weren't ready to soar high. Instead they were drowning, and when drowning, you need to calm down and find a way to float. That's what Knudstorp focused everyone's attention on; they needed to get stable. According to Knudstorp, a stable company may expand every three to five years into a new industry, learning to master it and improving over time. LEGO spread its attention into five new areas every year and failed at all of them.

To become profitable again, they got rid of the money-losing theme parks and games, reduced their product lines by about 30 percent to ones that were profitable, eliminated about half the kind of bricks that they make, and ensured that retailers were making big margins so stores would want to carry the product. They had to get back to basics and focus their attention on the here and now.

The impact was immediately felt. The company went from losing hundreds of millions a year to being profitable and doing a billion dollars in revenue in 2005. In the years that followed the company kept doubling sales every few years, and as of this writing it is now selling almost $10 billion in bricks and products. What Knudstorp and the leadership team did to unlock the company's success was give them the gift of focus, the constraints of profitability, and the simplicity of letting them know what to use their attention on, when, and how.

But the changes to the culture extended even further. The company developed new review processes and standards for making sets profitable. Possibly one of the most interesting traditions that was introduced is a fireside. Anyone at the company can request a fireside at any time. When they do, everyone they invite gathers and quietly listens to the speaker's ideas or concerns but is not allowed to respond. The speaker is given their full attention. LEGO trusts its people so much that if any of them feel there is an issue or concern, they can take everyone's time and attention as needed so that, as a company, they don't make the mistakes that almost doomed them during the early 2000s.

And here lies the second pillar of team intelligence . . . attention.

For a team or organization to be effective, we need to know what to pay attention to and when. LEGO almost failed because it couldn't direct its attention long enough to make anything new succeed. It was all over the place, but once it had a clear strategy for focusing people, and letting them get the work done, they unlocked incredible results.

Shifting Your Attention

When researcher Anita Williams Woolley, whom we met in the last chapter, examined teams with high intelligence, she found very clear patterns. These teams managed to synchronize when they worked, what they worked on, and even the way they talked. They had "bursty" communication, conversational turn-taking, high psychological safety, and even specific team gender ratios.

Bursty Communication
Woolley found that the most effective teams communicated in bursts. They came together, talked, settled on a solution, defined their next steps, and then went to work on their own, uninterrupted. They were masterful at synchronizing and directing their attention. When they were together, they came to clear conclusions so that people knew what work had to be done next, and so when they were apart, they rarely needed to interrupt each other to get more information. We know that if you want to make the team stupider, constantly distract everyone. Protecting our attention is hard in the modern workplace, especially with all the communication apps we use constantly going off. I'm not making a dig at texting, Slack, or Teams. I think they are great products, but we need an etiquette for how to use them—we need an Emily Post for the twenty-first century.

At LEGO before Knudstorp took over, teams were all over the place. Some teams never met even though they were working on the same project. They may have been working uninterrupted, but if they didn't agree on what to focus on, they were probably working on the wrong thing and inevitably there would be massive conflicts when they delivered. On the other extreme, the company as a whole couldn't focus. They were spread across so many projects that they were constantly distracting themselves with a new failed launch. For bursty communication to work, you need to balance getting everyone communicating to clarify what to focus on and then giving them the time to deliver. Nonstop communication is distracting, and never meeting leads to conflicts and wasted work. Teams need a balance.

Synchronized Behaviors and Thinking

Teams that performed better were not only syncing up in their communications, but Woolley found that they were also in sync with respect to their facial expressions and emotional states. That's because when we are both paying attention to the same material and are engrossed in it, our brain waves begin to align. In neuroscience, this is known as neural entrainment. You have probably experienced working with people and being so in sync that you develop a shorthand of signals, personal jokes, or phrases that let you work much faster together.

Conversational Turn-Taking

One clue that people are synchronized and are using their attention effectively is that throughout a project, everyone on the team talks about it equally. It can be over email, virtual meetings, software like Slack or Teams, or in person; it's called conversational turn-taking. This doesn't mean it is equal at every meeting, so you don't need to get self-conscious if you are presenting for most of a meeting, but it does average out over a project. What it does mean is that we need to encourage the quieter people to share more. Just because someone is louder doesn't make them smarter, and the simple fact that someone is quiet doesn't mean they have nothing to share.

The Mind in the Eyes

It turns out that when Woolley compared different predictors of effective teams, she discovered something unexpected: There is one thing that underpins all the elements of attention. It is also the single greatest predictor of team intelligence, and every woman reading this will respond with "Yah, obviously."

The predictor was the number of women on the team. It wasn't enough for a team to have one woman; the gain started at two and grew with the number of women until there was only one man on the team. Groups composed entirely of women underperformed versus mixed groups. This raises several questions, among them, What do women do that adds so much to team intelligence, and why does a team need more than one but less than all?

The answer may lie with Borat's family, and yes, I'm talking about the cousin of actor and comedian Sacha Baron-Cohen. Sir Simon Philip Baron-Cohen didn't go into comedy but instead became a highly respected clinical psychologist who has been studying autism for decades. He developed a theory called mind blindness. By the age of five, most of us understand that other people have emotions that are different than ours, and we learn to read their emotions by observing their behavior, body language, and facial expressions. This ability to understand that other people have different perspectives and ways of thinking than our own is called theory of mind. (*Borat voice*) And this theory is VERY NICE!

When we see someone slumped over, sitting by themselves, our first assumption is not "Wow, they must be really happy," because we understand those signals. But Sir Baron-Cohen noticed that people with autism spectrum disorder have a delay in their ability to read those signals and to intuit what is going on in other people's minds. They have mind blindness.

Baron-Cohen created a test called "Reading the Mind in the Eyes,"

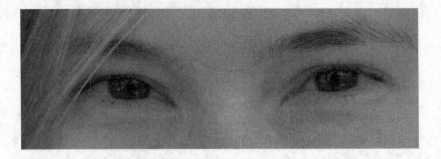

where people are shown black-and-white photos of eyes and have to guess what emotion the person was experiencing.

Here is a little quiz for you. What emotion do these eyes demonstrate?

Do you think this woman is:

A.   Playful
B.   Comforting
C.   Irritated
D.   Bored
E.   Wondering how many copies of this book you got for your organization

Although the test was created to understand autism, it's also useful for measuring people's emotional intelligence or mind-reading abilities. It evaluates how good you are at putting yourself in someone else's shoes and seeing the world through their eyes; essentially, it tests your empathy.

If you picked Answer A, "Playful," you are right, and here is why it's important for creating super teams.

The biggest benefit of having a team of mostly women came from the fact that women tend to score higher than men on theory-of-mind activities. Ultimately, if you want to create a super team, they need to interact, and assuming people are generally competent, what unlocks a team's ability to work is having members who score high in emotional intelligence regardless of their gender identity.

Think about it like this: You are in a meeting, and your overconfident boss is giving another famously long monologue as if he's the lead in a community production of *Hamlet*. Your coworker Mary tries to signal for attention and makes a face, but he doesn't notice. Because of your high emotional intelligence, you see the signal and interrupt on her behalf, saying, "I think Mary has some thoughts on this." Now the team can benefit from Mary's contributions and your boss won't be stuck in an echo chamber, missing blind spots, like the fact that he's boring and bad at public speaking.

High emotional intelligence lets people understand when to push on a topic and when it's not the best time; it helps them determine how to share an idea so that people can hear it and sense whether a topic is sensitive and should be avoided. In this way, emotional intelligence unlocks attention. It allows people to navigate the complexities of interpersonal relationships and enhance the group's psychological safety. Sound familiar? Yah, because it feels like we are describing our favorite glue player, Shane Battier. Because Shane had both clear alignment on the goal of having the team win and high emotional intelligence, he could help the team work better together. Remember what Morey said about him: they called him LEGO because when he was on the court, everyone would click into place. He also shared that Battier would communicate more with his teammates than anyone else. He would create communication bursts on the court so that they would focus on the right things. And, much like Knudstorp joining LEGO, when LEGO joined the Heat, team intelligence grew and the results skyrocketed.

I would bet that if Shane took a theory-of-mind test he would have a very high score. Although scoring well on a test doesn't solve everything, a team made up of low-scoring people will probably struggle even more to find ways to connect with each other, synthesize different perspectives, and develop new ways to solve problems. Put simply, they will have a hard time directing their attention, since the team dynamic may feel jumpy, erratic, and out of whack. It is similar to what happened at LEGO before Knudstorp, when people tried to bring up problems with the new products; leadership used fear and threats to quiet dissent rather than acknowledging the considerations and engaging with people who so clearly cared about the success of the mission.

Psychological Safety

Just like *chillax*, *SEO*, and *virality*, *psychological safety* became a big buzzword in the business world in the early 2000s when Amy Edmondson released a paper asking what predicts team success. Her conclusion was backed by several other studies, including the now-famous Project Aristotle from Google. After reviewing hundreds of teams at Google, researchers found that success didn't depend on common hobbies, if people socialized together, how many years people had worked together, seniority, how extroverted they were, or individual performance. Instead it came from what Edmondson described as "a sense of confidence that the team will not embarrass, reject, or punish someone for speaking up. This confidence stems from mutual respect and trust among team members."

In other words, you can't get people reasoning effectively or direct their attention well if they are too scared to speak. When people feel safe enough to share their ideas and challenge other people's ideas, the communication can be synchronized and bursty. If they don't feel safe, then you have authoritarianism, which is generally dysfunctional, ineffective, and, most importantly, not fun. Stalin? Mussolini? Bad bosses, worse hangs. People can pitch a half-baked idea and even if doesn't work, it can inspire other people on the team, but if people are too scared to share, we lose their contributions.

Often when people hear about the concept of psychological safety, they imagine a team where everyone is holding hands and singing together. That's not psychological safety; that sounds more like a drug-induced personal development journey that rich tech people do on vacation in Tulum, Mexico. There is nothing wrong with that, but it's just not what creates a super team with high intelligence. As author Shane Snow points out in his book *Dream Teams*, teams with high psychological safety have higher rates of conflict. If you are too scared to disagree with your coworkers or boss, you will stay quiet and there will be no conflict. But you will also make terrible decisions because no one challenges the quality of the ideas or points out the flaws. People and ideas can't improve without feedback. One study on nurses found that the teams with higher rates of psychological safety actually reported more potential safety issues. The fact is, if you are scared you will get fired, you will stay quiet, but if you know you are safe, you will report the issue and can improve.

When teammates feel safe to voice their opinions, not only do you have more ideas to pick from, but you will also have more feedback to improve. Sometimes as ideas push against each other, there will be conflict, and that's a good thing, as long as the arguments don't get personal.

We are used to thinking of ideas and teams as either fragile—they break easily like a drink glass hitting the floor—or robust—the ideas or team are tough and can handle anything. Instead, there's a third category, known as anti-fragile. These are things that, when you apply pressure to them, get stronger. It's like weight lifting. When you pick up the right amount of weight, the pressure causes the muscles to tear and then grow back stronger. The same is true for ideas and teams. When you put the right amount of pressure on them through feedback, both the ideas and the teams get totally ripped. The feedback lets you see the flaws and fix them. When psychological safety is high, you may have higher rates of conflict, but that means that the ideas and the team will get stronger. This is what bursty communication is all about. The team will come together, work through ideas, push on them, find the flaws, and define next steps, so that everyone is synchronized and can do their part.

Think back to LEGO's challenges. Teams were working in parallel but never communicating; they were doubling the work and producing a failed product. What they needed was open, bursty communication.

Fundamentally, team intelligence thrives when people and teams synchronize their strategies and communication. You can have perfect alignment around your goals, but if everyone on the team is using different strategies to get there and is distracting each other by communicating at random times, the team will get stupider.

Even with all these insights, there are still two questions: Why doesn't it help to only have one woman, and why do you need at least one man? The answers to both are explained by the third pillar of team intelligence: resources. To understand that, let's look at a group of experts and their adventures in the quaint city of Antwerp, Belgium.

Ideas in Action

Focusing the team's attention is critical, and to do that you have several options:

- *Bursty communication:* We need to agree on when we focus our group attention and on what.
  - *Set times for bursts:* Schedule time for people to connect, ask questions, and define next steps. That can sometimes be impromptu when you are on deadline but avoid continuous communication if you can. That may mean setting rules for Slack and Teams and possibly creating an emergency channel to be answered immediately versus a general channel that can be answered when people are available.
  - *Define your communication methods and stick to them:* If you ask your team how they would set up a meeting, you will probably get a bunch of different answers, from texting people for the best time, emailing everyone, and assigning it based on looking at calendars, to posting to Teams or Slack or even messaging an admin to make it happen. If that one action has so many answers across so many platforms, it means that there is no standardized communication system. You need to make the implicit explicit. Each platform has a specific use. You don't use a stake to kill a werewolf, but you can use a steak to distract one while you get away. Using the wrong tool makes a mess and increases team stupidity. Have a standard protocol like:
    - Slack/Teams: General internal group discussion
    - Email: Connecting with outside vendors and customers

- Texting: Absolute emergencies
- Audio-video recordings: Passing summaries or updates
- Central file server: Storing all files from every project so there is a record of all work and documentation

  - *Make communication more difficult:* This sounds counterintuitive, but when communication is too easy, everyone is constantly distracted. Most answers could be found without distracting someone else. There is a difference between asking for help and distracting someone because you don't want to bother finding the file yourself. I know that navigating the unwieldy jungle of shared file drives is thankless work, but take the extra two minutes and track it down rather than distracting people with more emails.
  - *This does NOT mean more meetings:* People confuse bursty communication with increasing the number of meetings; it does not mean that. It is about getting everything synchronized at the meetings so you can work uninterrupted afterward. At some companies I work with we have the "Necessity Rule": if it isn't necessary to have a meeting, it is necessary *not* to, and if it isn't necessary to have someone at the meeting, it is necessary *not* to. We need to give people more undistracted work time.

- *Synchronization:* Let's make the implicit explicit so that we can sync, and so our attention is on the same things.

- *Track communications frequency:* Teams that have the highest intelligence communicate close to equally over a project. To support you and your team, you can use tools and software built into most platforms that track people's communication. It will usually mean encouraging the quieter people to speak up. An important note: Although some people are good at speaking off the cuff, many aren't. You didn't hire your people because they are good at improvising, because if you have ever seen improv you know no one is good at improvising. So, if you want people's opinions at meetings, and your employees haven't been trained at Second City or another improv comedy institution, you may want to send them material ahead of time to review.
- *Test your team's emotional intelligence:* You can find out how empathetic your team is and strengthen the skill over time. Links to the test are available on my website: www.JonLevy.com. When you know who performs well, invite them to support group attention, and help people who are quieter speak up more and share.

- *Psychological safety:* Let's make it safe to speak up.
  - *Request dissenting views:* In a meeting ask the team the following (and when someone answers, listen, thank them for their ideas, and explore them if they are relevant):
    - What am I missing here?
    - What is the flaw with this idea?
    - When we look back, what will we have said caused us to fail?

- *Differentiate useful conflict from abuse:* If what people say moves the conversation forward, it is useful. If they are just trash-talking a person or repeating ideas that don't improve anything, then your work culture is a high school lunchroom at best, abusive at worst. If people feel shame for sharing an idea, they won't continue, and if an argument becomes personal it is no longer useful. An example: "The problem is that Miguel never thinks through these things." This was a direct attack; it was destructive. The person could have said, "Miguel, that's an interesting idea. Have you thought through how we would handle these situations?" This is constructive. You reveal the weaknesses in the idea so they can be improved, or the team can move on to another idea.

- *Giving status:* Here are a few ways you can reward habits that create attention:
    - *Celebrate uninterrupted time:* Highlight all the work that people have been able to do without interruption.
    - *Pay attention to new shorthand:* Call out new catchphrases and shorthand that accelerate communication.
    - *Track and address conversational turn-taking:* Highlight when people have equal or near equal rates, and address when you see groups under-indexing. Speak to the quieter people and encourage them. Also have a direct conversation with the extroverts about giving space for others and supporting the introverts.

- *Empower those with more emotional intelligence:* Have the people who can read the room better support more effective meetings and team dynamics.
- *Acknowledge sharing of problems:* If people are scared to share problems, they will keep great ideas to themselves. Reinforce the behavior that it is good to be open. Compliment people publicly for sharing bad news.

Chapter 8

Team Intelligence—Resources

On February 16, 2003, Leonardo Notarbartolo walked into his office for the last time. He worked in the diamond quarter of Antwerp, Belgium, a small three-square-block area through which an estimated 80 percent of the world's rough diamonds flow. His office was in the heart of the Diamond Quarter, at the Antwerp Diamond Center, a set of three interconnected office buildings. Hidden two stories below the second building sat a vault that was believed to store more than $100 million worth of jewels and cash. It was supposed to be impenetrable, especially since, in addition to the ten layers of vault security, guards, and gates, the Diamond Quarter is under twenty-four-hour police surveillance and monitored by sixty-three cameras. It's like a turducken of security; under each layer is a new and bigger challenge, and even though it might look mouthwatering, few people have the stomach to handle all of it.

In the summer of 2001, Leonardo was sitting at a café when he was approached by a longtime colleague and fellow gems dealer. The man had a single question for Notarbartolo, and if he could answer it, Leonardo would be given 100,000 euros: Could the vault in the Antwerp Diamond Center be robbed?

For this to make sense, it would help to know two things. The first is that Leonardo did deal in gems, but he sourced them the way that pirates sourced treasures: by stealing them. He was a world-class thief who would sell his prizes to local diamond dealers. The second is that he kept his own diamonds in that vault, so he knew how tight the security was.

Being a professional, he wanted to, as they say in the movies, "case the joint" to make sure. So, to do reconnaissance, he entered the vault carrying a pen cam in his pocket. What he found was that the vault was protected by ten layers of security, including a magnetic field, a seismic sensor, a Doppler radar, infrared heat detectors, a footlong key, not to mention a lock with a four-number combination (100 million possible codes). Once inside, each safe-deposit box required two keys and a combination lock with over 17,500 possibilities.

Although Leonardo had a particular set of skills, this caper was far beyond his expertise. Leonardo was a social engineer; he knew how to charm people to get access to places and things he shouldn't. For example, he would claim that he wanted more storage space in the vault to convince the building to let him see its schematics. He was great at gathering information, but for a high-risk and complex job like this, he would need a team of experts. This is where the story diverges depending on who tells it. There are two different accounts of what happens next.

The first is that back in his thirties, when he lived outside Turin, Italy, Leonardo made it his job to know people with every talent imaginable, from safecrackers and tunneling experts to master lockpickers and people who could scale walls. They were known as the School of Turin. Depending on the heist, he would pick the talent with the right skills.

But in an interview with *Wired* magazine, Notarbartolo claimed that he told the businessman it was impossible, and delivered the photos and intel. Five months later he was asked to meet up again with the businessman, this time at an address outside Antwerp. There he encountered a group of men, and a life-size replica of the safe built to exact dimensions based on the photos and schematics he had previously shared. Regardless of which version, if any, of the story is true, Leonard now had his crew:

- *The Monster:* He had this name because he was "monstrously good at everything he did," including picking locks, electrical work, mechanics, and brute strength.

- *The Genius:* He was the tech expert on the team specializing in disabling the alarm systems.

- *The King of Keys:* You would have thought he was a crew member's grandfather, but this older man was one of the best key forgers in the world. He was to duplicate the foot-long key they would need to unlock the vault.

The King of Keys requested a clear video of the key from Leonardo. When Leonardo explained it would not be easy to get, the Genius chimed in, "Don't worry, I'll help." Because each team member was clear on everyone else's skills and specialties, they knew whom to go to for what task. No one would have expected the Monster to charm the building staff or the Genius to forge the key.

In the coming months, the pieces began to fall into place, allowing the team to break down layer after layer of security. Leonardo managed to place a thumbnail-sized camera above the combination lock, so that as security opened the safe, it provided a clear view of both the combination and the key as it was inserted. To pick up the signal, the team installed a fully functioning fire extinguisher in a nearby storage room with a hidden compartment that could record the signal. To get past the motion and heat sensors, they realized they could use women's hair spray to temporarily block the signal.

With the addition of Speedy, their getaway driver, the team was complete, and the evening before the heist they celebrated with dinner at their hideout.

The next night, the heist was on. The King of Keys picked a lock to a building behind the Antwerp Diamond Center. Now in the adjoining courtyard, they had to get past thermal and motion sensors, so the Monster slowly approached using a large polyester sheet to diffuse the heat and then placed a shield in front of the sensor, so they were free to move around. After the Genius disabled the entry alarm, they went down into the building, covering cameras with bags, before finally arriving in front of the vault.

The Genius managed to use a special aluminum tool he had developed to override the magnetic signal, and before the King of Keys tried his forgery, he had a hunch. In the videos, security would always go to a nearby closet and come back with the key. So, looking in the closet, he found the original key, slipped it in, entered the combination, and opened the safe.

Using the hair-spray technique the Monster entered the vault, carefully found the wires feeding the sensors, and bypassed them. Everything was going according to plan. They could now get to work without the risk of setting off the alarms. The King of Keys pulled out a homemade nose puller, a device that would attach to a safe-deposit box lock, and after a few minutes of twisting, pop it open.

Having practiced on the replica safe, they could work almost entirely in the dark, only occasionally flashing a light long enough to position the nose puller. In those brief glimpses, they could see the incredible score they were taking home, from cash and gold bars to satchels and gem bags.

By 5:30 a.m. they had cleared 109 of the boxes, and it was time for them to make their getaway with what they estimated was the heist of the century, worth north of $100 million. It took more than an hour to move the duffel bags to the car and grab the tapes from the security room, but once they did, Speedy drove off with the loot and the other four men walked to Leonardo's home.

A few hours later, Notarbartolo and Speedy were off to Italy, a country with no extradition treaty, to live out their years as wealthy criminals who had pulled off the heist of the century . . . or that's what I would have said if Leonardo had read the first part of this book.

Indeed, the crew *had* pulled off the heist of the century and got away with it. But do you remember a few chapters back, when I explained that at a certain point, more talent isn't that helpful, and that what you really have to watch out for is incompetence? You can be the greatest cyclist in the world, but if your support person forgets to inflate your tires, there is no way you will win the race.

In heist movies, the cliché is that the last-minute addition to the crew brings them all down. It seems that life imitates art, because while Speedy may have been a great last-minute driver, he didn't have the nerves to handle the crime. He was outsmarted not by meddling kids and their dog, but rather—I kid you not—by an old man and his two pet ferrets named Mickey and Minnie.

The last stage of the plan involved Speedy and Leonardo driving to Italy. When they crossed the border between Belgium and France, they were supposed to pull off the highway and burn evidence like the security tapes, fake paperwork, meal receipts, plans, etc.

Unfortunately, while still in Belgium, Speedy was having a full-blown panic attack. Terrified that they were going to get caught at any minute, he demanded that they pull over and get rid of the evidence right then and there. Leonardo found an off-ramp and went to find a suitable burning site, but when he got back, Speedy had gone off the deep end, just throwing the tapes, papers, and evidence over some trail. Leonardo was in shock, so with no way to find everything in the dark, he helped Speedy spread it all out, hoping that everything would break down and be destroyed by nature. They sped off to Italy thinking they had done their job.

What Leonardo and Speedy could have never imagined was that this trail was owned by an elderly man who took frequent walks with his ferrets, a man who had a habit of calling the police anytime someone threw trash on his property. When the old man mentioned to the authorities that the words ANTWERP DIAMOND CENTER were printed on some envelopes, the police swarmed the area and pulled everything into evidence. The evidence led police to Leonardo, the Monster, the Genius, and Speedy, but none of them knew that yet. So Leonardo did something even more clichéd than adding someone to the crew last minute. Instead of staying in Italy, a country with no extradition agreement with Belgium, he decided to go back to the scene of the crime and visit his office. When he arrived, the police quickly took him into custody.

They had gotten away with the greatest diamond robbery ever, but hubris and an acceptance of incompetence ultimately brought them down.

To this day the ringleader and the King of Keys have never been arrested, and the assets were never recovered. What happened to them, we may never know. Notarbartolo claims that when the crew made it home to unpack the loot, satchel after satchel was empty. What should have been $100 million was more like $20 million. He may have found himself in the middle of an elaborate insurance fraud, where he had been tricked into robbing an almost empty safe so that the ringleader and his diamond-dealing friends could collect insurance money while still keeping their product. It is also possible that Notarbartolo has it all hidden away someplace, waiting for the day he can collect it.

Resources

So, what can we learn from this story? Most importantly, never trust the last-minute addition to a heist crew, and never return to the crime scene. Besides those clichés, it seems that achieving what most people think is impossible is more about having the team with the right resources. Leonardo would never have been able to get into that safe on his own, because he didn't have the necessary knowledge, skills, experience, mental models, or tools.

It was only because each of the members of the crew had unique knowledge, and everyone on the team was clear what people's specialties were, that they were able to pull it off—up until Speedy's lack of nerve, which brought the entire scheme down. A team made up solely of technical experts like the Genius wouldn't have been able to accomplish the heist of the century because they wouldn't have had the social engineering or the key-making skills. It was because each of the team members had different knowledge and skills that the plan succeeded at all.

In scientific papers, researchers call it memory, and they don't mean storing random facts in your head for trivia night. It's about what the team members know, how they think, what skills they have, and how you access them. Put simply, it's about diverse and complementary resources—human resources, yes, that combine to form the third pillar of team intelligence.

A Big Toolbox

You can't build a house with just screwdrivers, and you can't mix a screwdriver only with orange juice. You see my point?

Your resources need to be diverse. You want hammers, saws, tape measures, glass cutters, rendering software, and the eccentric host of an HGTV show. This is what we mean by diversity of resources. In the US when we hear the word *diversity*, people often think about how many people of color there are on a team, or if there is trans or disabled representation, and yes, that's important, but the diversity that I'm referring to here is broader.

Let's use a trivia example: If all team members are music experts, the team won't be great at sports or political questions. With each additional person who knows about music, you are not adding new resources to the team. It's like adding a hundredth screwdriver to your toolbox. It doesn't help; you are just adding overlapping resources. What we want is people who have a diverse knowledge going across history, pop culture, politics, sports, etc.

But diversity doesn't stop there. It also includes having diverse skills. You don't want to launch a financial services app if all you have is a team of finance experts. You need programmers, designers, salespeople, marketers, a King of Keys, a Monster, a social engineer—oh, wait, those last three are just for heists. Woolley took the idea of diversity one step further, to the way we think; her research found that teams made up of people who think differently (they have different cognitive styles) far outperform other groups. For example, when teams combine people who are great at spatial visualization—they tend to be good at math and navigation—with those who are strong at object visualization—artists and designers—and add people with high verbal skills—the types who organize the world in words instead of pictures—these teams have very high intelligence. That's because they are increasing the total diversity of resources.

This shouldn't surprise us, that with each new skill and perspective, we are adding a tool that can help us succeed. At my first job, my boss would tell me that if we agree on everything, one of us isn't necessary, and that's the point. We need different resources from our team members, or they aren't adding anything; they're just eating break-room cookies that should rightfully go to me.

How does gender diversity figure into this discussion? As I explained in Chapter 7, teams benefit from having more than one woman in the group. One reason is the ally effect. Women in the business world often share that they are ignored or don't feel comfortable speaking up when they don't have another woman as an ally in the environment. Meanwhile, men have the tendency to speak regardless of whether they are the only man in the room. That's why having even one man join a group of women increases team intelligence, but we often need two women on a team to experience a bump. Once again, psychological safety—or the lack thereof—rears its head. When people don't feel safe, or experience being ignored, they don't speak up, and we lose the value of their resources. We would probably experience a gain with only one woman if we could ensure that the men in the room have a high level of social intelligence and function as allies.

At this point, some people might say, "Wouldn't a team be more diverse if we added a tightrope walker, to a group of programmers?" The answer is, I don't know. It depends on what the person's other skills are; no person is just one thing. The tightrope walker may bring other resources, like being an incredible marketer or project manager, or having the emotional intelligence to walk the thin line between giving useful feedback and insulting people.

It's important that we realize that diversity goes beyond the easy-to-see factors of race or gender. Part of the benefit of racial diversity is that people from different cultures come with different life experiences and add unique value to the group's resources. I know it is a subject that people have a lot of feelings and opinions about, so please hear me out. Saying I need to hire three people of a specific race can sound more than a little weird.

Instead, consider that someone who comes from a different race, ethnicity, gender, or religion has lived a very different life than the other people on the team. This means they have unique resources in the form of knowledge, mental models, memories, perspectives, preferences, and contacts that the rest of the team doesn't have, and as a result, the team gets more intelligent from those resources. Like Daryl Morey did when he was looking for talent and found Shane Battier, we need to look past the obvious characteristics like race and gender and look for the characteristics of diversity that add resources to the team, or else we miss the point. I want a diverse team, because I get more resources, and those resources often come because people have had different lived experiences that are informed by gender, race, etc. It seems so strange to keep reducing people to their race and gender, rather than looking at the breadth of the resources they add. Currently, when we hear someone being called a diversity hire, it suggests the person is not qualified and were only hired to fulfill some gender or race quota. Most people don't want to be hired because of a quota; we want to be hired because we are competent and skilled. Instead, if we focus on the resources people bring, and the team is explicitly made aware of them, then they will get excited for the new skills, contacts, and expertise that the person brings. What we want is a diversity hire, when it is a diversity of resources. I said it before, and I'll say it again: we need to move past what is easy to measure and start measuring what is useful.

This brings us back to the idea that teams with high intelligence make the implicit explicit. Remember when the crew from the Antwerp diamond heist came together? They openly shared their expertise, what they knew and didn't know—and what they needed to learn to be successful. When the King of Keys said he needed a video of the vault key, and Leonardo said he didn't know how to get that, the Genius chimed in with ideas. Everyone knew who had what information and skills, and this was reinforced with months of practicing together.

To unlock a team's intelligence, it is important that the team members openly talk about the resources they have. They let each other know what topics they are experts at, what ways they work best, how they think, what kind of work they have done in the past, where they have contacts and relationships, etc. They pair this with an organized information system. For example, they keep all files on a shared drive that is organized and labeled so that work doesn't turn into a document scavenger hunt. Now when people need to figure out a solution, they know where to find files (they don't distract each other needlessly), and they know who to go to, to leverage the right resources.

We finally have a full picture of what leads to team intelligence, and of what, when done wrong, produces team stupidity.

Intelligent teams apply habits consistent with all three pillars:

1. *Reasoning:* They have full alignment on their objectives, from the larger company goal down to the team and personal goals.

2. *Attention:* They know what to pay attention to, when, and how. Supported by emotional intelligence, they have bursty communication, high psychological safety, and conversational turn-taking.

3. *Resources:* They are a team with diverse resources, and they have made the implicit explicit. Everyone knows what their teammates can provide, and where to find and access shared resources.

So, what should leaders and teams do when it comes to resources?

Ideas in Action

In most cases you won't be able to hire a bunch of people onto the team to increase resources, so we need to work with what we have. How do we maximize our talent?

- *Catalog your resources:* You can't use something if you don't know you have it or you don't know where to find it. So, the first step is to make the implicit explicit. We need each team member to list their:
  - *Super skills:* Where do you shine, what is your combination of skills that are just outstanding?
  - *Knowledge:* What experiences, mental models, and expertise do you have? This is about what you know and how you think about it.
  - *Access:* Share who you know and where you can go. This isn't about name-dropping; it is about what resources would be useful. If you are on a lobbying team and your uncle is a high-ranking official, you may want to mention it; the same if you went to school with someone useful.
  - *Physical resources:* What you have that could be useful; for example, you have a big van so your band can tour.
  - *Best work hours:* Some people need to put their kids to bed so early evening isn't great; others are prepping for a triathlon so early mornings aren't great. It is absolutely fair to let people know your nonnegotiables.
  - *Pitfalls:* Call yourself out on areas you need support. For example, I sometimes don't share in a meeting unless someone directly asks, so please ask often. Or I give the best feedback if I have materials

a couple of days before a meeting so I can review and do a deep dive. I shared that I have a learning disability; don't come to me for spell-check.

Ideally, when we start a project, we share these, so everyone gets to know each other's resources. You will notice that just doing this exercise will inspire new solutions and options. People forget the incredible breadth of resources they have and are surprised when they discover what other people know and can contribute.

- *Create player cards or docs:* Turn people's resource lists into playing cards, like kids collect of Pokémon or their favorite athletes. This way, anytime someone joins the team they can quickly review the cards and understand what resources the team has, and everyone can read the new person's card and find out what was added. I would also invite them to add a few personal fun facts. In my case, I would share:
    - I have traveled to all seven continents and did it in eight months.
    - I was once crushed by a bull in Pamplona and almost died.
    - I battled Kiefer Sutherland in drunken Jenga and won an invite to his family Thanksgiving, but when I showed up, he had been so drunk he forgot. It was very awkward, but he still honored the invite.

When people share a bit about their life, it humanizes them and makes them more dynamic in the eyes of their team members. It also provides a starting point for "get to know you" conversations.

- *Organize your files:* Let's make this simple. Most teams have terrible information hygiene. They store files and information across personal computers, email inboxes, shared servers, and text messages, just to name a few. In fact, one study suggests office workers spend four hours a day just looking for the document they need to work on. Okay, so this is a stat I made up. But be honest: you were ready to believe it because it feels true. Bad information hygiene makes us much stupider. Taking the extra minute to file things in the right places makes everyone else's life far easier, including my own when I need to find something. We have to organize information so it is easy to retrieve. This is another example of how when we focus only on ourselves by putting things only where we want them to go, it costs the team and lowers its intelligence.

- *Encourage people to explore:* If you can't add people to the team that make your resources more diverse, encourage your team to explore new ideas. Either ask people to volunteer to learn about a subject or provide company-paid classes in different topics. This can be anything from the cool trending innovation in the industry to basic skills like writing, pitching, or design. Alternatively, you can have a team book club or offer to expense books on different topics. You might even recommend a certain business advice book from a dashingly handsome, endlessly witty, and charismatic young author. Or if they have read that book, you could recommend mine. These kinds of habits don't only increase resources, but they encourage a growth mindset.

- *Hire for diversity:* If the opportunity to hire someone to the team comes along, have applicants fill out the same player card that you have your own people fill out. You can anonymize them and see which resources would be most useful to the team. This way you can focus on candidates who increase the total relevant resources of the group. The emphasis is on the relevant part, so if you run a marketing agency, it might be useful to hire a former magazine publisher since they have different contacts and perspectives, but chances are it probably won't make sense to hire a former ghost hunter since your office isn't haunted.

- *Highlight generosity:* When team members share resources toward a common goal, make sure to note that in front of everyone. Find reasons to acknowledge everyone for their generosity so as to reinforce the behavior.

- *Acknowledge new resources:* When people develop a new skill, knowledge, contacts, etc., talk about it at meetings the same way you emphasize the variety of skills someone new brings to the team. You might even update their card to reflect this new skill.

- *Compliment file use:* Reward and acknowledge the team for keeping files organized and up-to-date. Celebrate it and even dedicate time to get it working, and set deadlines for updates so your files don't look like a messy desktop. Even create catchphrases around it like "It's filed, or it didn't happen," "A project isn't real until it's filed," or "People who care about their team file their docs." That one is a bit manipulative, but it gets the point across.

Chapter 9
The Good and the Bad

So far, I've mostly been pointing out the upside of human behavior—all the ways in which selflessness, collaboration, trust, emotional intelligence, and other "prosocial" behaviors benefit individuals, teams, and organizations. I've been encouraging you not to fixate on only recruiting star talent, but rather to recognize, support, and reward the contributions that different kinds of team members make, often with little notice, to an organization's success. How do we spot glue players like Shane Battier? How do we reward them? We'll turn to that in a minute.

But I would be irresponsible if I didn't acknowledge a harsh reality—the fact that far too many workplaces and organizations are populated by people whose better angels flew the coop long ago, if they were ever present in the first place. I have a feeling you know just what I'm talking about—those bad actors who do more harm than good. I need to make sure you know how to navigate both the good and the bad. Let's start with the bad.

Toxic Messes

In Chapter 3, I emphasized that accentuating the positives won't be enough to stop the harm that negative behaviors unleash on teams and organizational culture. The negative impact of a toxic personality is much worse than the positive impact of organized files and friendly chitchat.

As much as we need to spot useful team members, we need to be on the lookout for what psychologists refers to as the Dark Tetrad, or a "dark personality." These are the people who treat others terribly for their own pleasure and rationalize it by viewing those they mistreat as somehow being below them. A dark personality sees themselves as better than others and so they justify doing what they want. In extreme cases, they treat coworkers like pawns in a game or act with revenge or cruelty. They may spread rumors and destroy careers, find a generous teammate and use them, take credit for all their work, or even be abusive. In the more subtle cases, these are people who actively undermine the group or its members and create nonproductive conflict. Just to be clear, someone disagreeing with the group and arguing for a strategy is not toxic; healthy debate is the sign of a healthy team and culture. What we are talking about is people who actively promote a personal agenda, at the cost of the group members. If we want to build smart teams with high intelligence, we need to understand whom not to engage with, or if we have no choice, how to protect ourselves from the Dark Tetrad.

Toxic characteristics exist on a spectrum from mild to extreme. It is important to differentiate someone acting selfish one time from consistently acting selfish, so we have to be careful not to label people too quickly or too categorically. Your coworker who stole your leftover salmon from the fridge is almost certainly not a psychopath. According to psychologist Delroy L. Paulhus and his colleagues, the Dark Tetrad consists of:

1. *Psychopathy:* Hollywood has us imagining charming serial killers like Charles Manson, Ted Bundy, or Hannibal Lecter. That's because psychopaths have impaired empathy or lack remorse. They don't feel bad for their behavior. What makes this really dangerous is that it is paired with a boldness or a lack of inhibition. Meaning, they will take big actions and not care about the effects on other people.

The terrifying part is that they have a superficial charm; so, they seem normal.
Put simply: They are bold, lack remorse, and seem charmingly normal.

2. *Narcissism:* This is an intense entitlement or selfishness that comes with a need for admiration and a lack of empathy. They feel that they are deserving of stardom, leadership, status, etc. and others should admire them, but they lack the emotional depth to empathize with others. As a result, they act entitled and superior to others. They might read this paragraph, and instead of feeling shame, they'll just be happy I'm talking about them.
Put simply: It's all about them.

3. *Machiavellianism:* People with this trait are often described as ruthless and cunning because others are just tools used to accomplish their own goals. They are chess masters, and we are just pawns to be played with and thrown aside until the next time they need us. The name comes from the author Niccolò Machiavelli, because of his book *The Prince*. In it, Machiavelli shares a series of lessons about a prince who takes for granted that any immoral act is justified to gain political success. Many people mistakenly think Machiavelli is the power-hungry one, which is just one of the many ways modern society has failed to learn the lessons of his book.
Put simply: They will use anyone or anything to get what they want; you are just a tool.

4. *Sadism:* These are the people who enjoy causing pain and suffering for others. It could be physical pain, like hitting a person, or emotional pain, like humiliation.
Put simply: They enjoy your suffering.

People with dark personalities sound absolutely terrifying. I feel like I just got a tour of a laboratory with the world's worst diseases, but instead of infecting bodies, they infect personalities. Any one of these would be damaging to a team's intelligence; a person with all of them would be absolutely destructive.

Psychopath

Research by Robert D. Hare suggests that about 1 percent of the population would fit the characteristics of a psychopath. But when it comes to senior businesspeople, the number is somewhere closer to 3–4 percent. Hare is famous for saying, "Not all psychopaths were in prison, some were in the boardroom." When researcher Kevin Dutton ran the Great British Psychopath Survey, he found that the professions with the most psychopaths were:

1. CEOs

2. Lawyers

3. Media people (TV and radio)

4. Salespeople

5. Surgeons

I should clarify, however, that the fact that someone has psychopathic tendencies doesn't mean they are a terrible human being. But it does mean that if their desires don't align with the group, it can be devastating.

Narcissist

In previous chapters we talked about the changes in the business world that lead people into the cult of self, so it's no surprise that, as some commentators have suggested, we are living through a narcissism epidemic. To survive any epidemic, we need to understand what it looks like, how common it is, and what to do or not do about it. Let's tackle how common it is first. The answer is, we don't know. Some estimate 0.5–5 percent of the population. Others studying narcissism as a trait believe problematic narcissism is as high as 10 percent of the population. Since it's a spectrum, it can be hard to give exact numbers.

One study examining narcissism from 1979 to 2006 found a 30 percent increase in narcissism scores among college students. In another study, adolescents agreeing with the statement "I am an important person" went from 12 percent in 1963 to 77–80 percent in 1992. In a review of 766,513 books between 1960 and 2008 the use of plural nouns like *we* and *us* decreased by 10 percent. Meanwhile, *I* and *me* increased by 42 percent. But what is really interesting is that *you* and *your* quadrupled.

Considering how common narcissism is, I want to make sure you understand that it is a lot like shoes. It comes in a variety of styles and sizes, and depending on who is wearing them it will really hurt when they step all over you. We are used to thinking of narcissists as attention-seeking, pretentious, arrogant, deeply insecure, bitter people, but it's more complex than that. The variations can be described in this way:

- *Grandiose:* They want fame, power, and admiration, and are often viewed as charming . . . don't be fooled. Their self-entitlement and lack of empathy means they exploit others and demonstrate aggressive and exhibitionist behaviors.

- *Vulnerable:* These are the classic incels and internet trolls. They may appear as shy or withdrawn, but when they don't get the attention they "deserve" they can become passive-aggressive or cast themselves as the victim to cope.

- *Communal:* These people pretend to be saviors or saints,

but they are just after attention and status and are often cruel to family and employees.

- *Antagonistic:* They are hypercompetitive, and view everyone as a rival that needs to be defeated. Unfortunately, it leads many to be top-performing super chickens.

- *Malignant:* These people show aggressive and vindictive behavior. If they think you have slighted them, they will take joy in embarrassing or punishing you.

- *Seductive:* You may recognize these people for their starring role in "The Worst Relationship You Ever Had." Joseph Burgo says they "understand... what makes other people 'tick,' and they use that knowledge to manipulate them."

I'll leave it to you to fill in the blank with your favorite variety of narcissist. But let's be clear: all of us have demonstrated some of these traits at some point in our lives. We have all met people that we think are awful, and don't deserve recognition or status. Being envious of them or relieved they are removed from positions of influence doesn't make you a narcissist, it makes you human. But if it is the way a person generally relates to life, that is a lot more concerning.

Narcissistic people tend to be masterful at arguing. They even have a special move, like some WWE wrestler, according to the psychologist Jennifer Freyd. It's called DARVO. Since they are so insecure, anything short of the admiration they feel they are entitled to is deemed an insult. If you call them out on being wrong, lying, breaking rules, or highlight an issue, they will DARVO you: Deny, Attack, Reverse Victim, and Offender. The RVO needs a little more explanation. This is when they make you the offender, the person who created the problem, and turn themselves into the victim of your or someone else's behavior.

Machiavellian

People who demonstrate Machiavellian traits are described as ruthless and cunning. At work this may look like a manager who constantly promises you a promotion if you work hard on the next project, but the promotion never comes. A coworker who gets everyone else to create the presentation and does nothing themselves, or gets you to share all of your knowledge and then pretends to be the expert, giving you no credit. Or a boss who tells you how much they respect and care about you every time they need your help, but when you need their support, they give an excuse. In short, they exploit. Identifying a Machiavellian is like finding Waldo: once you spot the striped-shirt little devil, you can't believe you didn't notice him before.

Reading this, you may be playing out conversations with your old bosses, coworkers, or even people who report to you, and you realize, wow, no wonder nothing I did worked to help them. Don't beat yourself up. (That's what sadists are for.) Unless, or even if you are a mental health professional, you probably wouldn't be able to do anything about it.

There is a quote misattributed to Winston Churchill: "You cannot reason with a tiger when your head is in its mouth." I think it captures the spirit of the situation perfectly.

Sadist

In the business context, sadists are terrifying personalities. They gain pleasure from making other people suffer and experience humiliation. This would be the boss who sets up an employee with an impossible deadline, so that they have an excuse to shame the person in front of the team for not accomplishing the work on time.

What Glows in the Dark

It would be nice to live in a world where abusive, malevolent people get what they deserve, but what we don't like to admit is that dark personalities can make people more successful *at times*. Does that mean you should become one? Absolutely not. But there are some situations in which it can be useful. According to research by the University of British Columbia psychologist Delroy Paulhus, "A job interview is one of the few social situations where narcissistic behaviours such as boasting actually create a positive impression. Normally, people are put off by such behaviour, especially over repeated exposure."

Since they are great at self-promotion and take credit for success, they will be more likely to be noticed and promoted, and get higher pay. According to Ramani Durvasula, "Narcissistic people on average tend to make more money, have greater career success, and are more likely to pursue and achieve positions of leadership. . . . Unfortunately, people are drawn to success and money." So that attention will only feed their narcissistic tendencies.

Meanwhile, it won't surprise you that a sadist who has some power would be able to keep people in line. It seems that most cult leaders, fascists, and dictators have found that even if they aren't sadists, having someone on the team who is can be a really effective way to suppress dissent. You may have noticed that it is much easier to achieve a goal if you manipulate everyone else to do the work. People who are Machiavellian can reach incredible heights, at least until they are found out. But even if they develop a reputation as manipulative, they can jump companies, where they get to start over somewhat, or if the results are good enough people will turn a blind eye. When it comes to psychopaths, something about their superficial charm and lack of remorse or empathy tends to keep getting them hired as corporate executives.

Toxic Cleanup

The difficulty with all of these dark personalities is that their skills, no matter how awful, can be very effective or useful. Steve Jobs was an incredible visionary, but he was also undeniably a narcissist. The problem emerged that Apple clearly did better as a company with him than without. When Apple tried to get rid of Steve, the company lacked direction and started falling apart. What we don't like to admit is that these situations are complicated; just because someone is toxic doesn't mean the company will part ways with them.

So, if we can't get rid of them, what can we do?

First of all, you need to identify that you are dealing with a toxic personality. You might be able to tell if someone is a narcissist because they will let you know how great they are, but the others are less obvious. A psychopath will likely make fast self-serving decisions, and not care about the impact on people's lives, or worse, enjoy the power they possess over them. Meanwhile, a Machiavellian may continuously make promises that don't come to life, and the sadist will always find a reason to punish people.

Rule No. 1: Do Not Call Them Out

Dark personalities tend to feel justified in the way they treat people, and often need to be the hero of their story. If you call them out, they will be pushed into a corner. Like a scared tiger they will be put on the defensive and you will start to look like lunch. They have a lot more experience being a dark personality than you do in dealing with one, so no matter how smart and capable you think you are, don't attack the tiger.

Find a Partner

Figuring this out on your own is tough. Not all charming people are psychopaths; there are plenty of charming jerks. So I recommend finding a trusted friend and doing occasional behavior checks. Tell them what happened and don't justify anyone's behavior. The problem with dark personalities is that they take advantage of our good nature. They will have us second-guess ourselves since the psychopath's superficial charm is very disarming, and you will think, *They care about me, they aren't so bad*, or the narcissist's DARVO will make us think we did something wrong. But that is just part of the way they manipulate people.

If you identify a pattern and have it well documented, or you see a risky scenario unfolding, you can go to HR. But remember, if the news has taught us anything, in most cases, HR's job is to protect the company, not you. If the person is more senior or highly valuable, the company priority may be to protect the valuable sadist rather than a junior associate they are abusing.

If you listen to self-declared social media experts, they will tell you to leave that toxic boss or work environment right away. But anyone who hands out advice like that clearly doesn't understand the complexities of real life. If your boss is a narcissist and you are depending on the job to support your family, you can't just quit and let your kids go hungry. You might have stock vesting that could be life-changing, or you might have the job you always wanted at the company of your dreams, so why should you have to leave because of them? Even if you do want to exit, a strategy can take months, so we want to focus on what's in our control.

Document Everything

Since people with dark personalities will manipulate, lie, ignore the truth, and retell history, you will need to be able to show a track record of behavior and breaches. Document everything and keep your own copies on your own computer that IT can't access (if you are legally allowed). This includes printing emails and text conversations.

In extreme cases, dark personalities have been known to delete and destroy other people's work so they can make colleagues and employees look bad, and then save the day because they "happen to have a backup." If you suspect that someone is functioning as a bad actor, you need to protect yourself. You might need to check with a lawyer, since it can get complicated if you are keeping company information. Depending on the impact the person is having on your life, it can be helpful to speak to a trained mental health expert to figure out the best strategies and how to protect yourself.

Part of the reason you need to have good documentation is to keep your sanity. They can be so convincing that you will begin to doubt your actions. Victims often question their own experience of life and can internalize the narrative that they are the issue; this is devastating. Having a documented history will protect you from falling into their trap. Also, if a situation ever develops where there is a legal issue or claim, you have a recorded history of behaviors, screenshots, files, etc. that you can duplicate and pass to your lawyer, HR, and others.

Limit Engagement

Like toxic waste or toxic exes, if you can put buffers between you and them it would be ideal. This might mean taking on projects that create distance or force boundaries. It is hard for them to require you to be at a meeting if you are on a flight, but that doesn't mean they won't lash out.

Create Transparency

It is much harder for someone to manipulate the team when we foster a culture of transparency and openness. Manipulative behavior thrives when people don't know what is going on. Teams should openly discuss workload and responsibilities at meetings. Make sure to point out any requests that go above and beyond and highlight patterns. It also helps to have allies on the team that protect each other, for example, "It seems that, Mike, you are asking Susan to pick up your extra work for the third time this month. I know that she is already working on a project with our group, and we are already overworked. I bet you can figure this out without her." Meanwhile, if you have a very secretive clicky culture, a dark personality can have people working against their own best interests, and for the manipulator's benefit.

Not to Sound Paranoid

The chances that any one person has characteristics consistent with the Dark Tetrad is low, but over the course of a career you will absolutely come across people who have at least some of them at some level. Dealing with these personalities is a career rite of passage, like missing a deadline, accidentally deleting a file, or lending $10,000 to a prince who emailed me saying he needs help (I'm expecting the money back any day). Now that you know what to look for, you will likely begin to see them more clearly. In most cases, you will probably be fine, but in the extreme cases you need to protect your career, and your mental health. Don't be afraid to talk to people. These personalities thrive when there is a lack of transparency, and people are scared to speak up.

This means that if you are assembling a team or hiring people, you want to avoid people who might have the characteristics of the Dark Tetrad and instead look for the people who have a positive impact on the team. These are the glue players, the ones who create connections between people and multiply their people's results.

How to Spot a Glue Player

As I've said way too many times at this point, a lot of companies fixate on recruiting star talent. If there is a salesperson who outsells everyone, we want them on the team. But what we almost never consider is if someone has a multiplier or spillover effect. These are the people who make their fellow teammates more valuable versus those who only have personal contributions. Organizations tend to assume that the most talented players will have the ability to inspire others and raise everyone else's game, and there is some truth to that. One study on cashiers found that if you have the most productive cashier in front of everyone, it causes the rest of the team to work faster and be more productive. A study on baseball players found that adding an effective batter to the team caused those who were batting ahead of him in the lineup to get easier pitches and perform better. But notice that in these examples, people aren't really working with each other—they are working *near* each other.

When we look at team dynamics, with high task interdependence, the data shows a different pattern. Joseph Price, a professor at Brigham

Young University and part of the National Bureau of Economic Research, and his collaborators were curious: Do other industries enjoy the benefit of multipliers, and if yes, how do they work? For example, does having a star player cause others to perform better, or are there other characteristics we should be looking at?

The researchers tried to simplify the question by looking at NBA players' salaries. What a player gets paid should represent what they contribute to the team through metrics like points, assists, blocks, etc., plus any impact they have on team members. Using a full season of play-by-play data and player stats, Price and his colleagues were able to find that players are almost exclusively paid on the easy-to-measure statistics. As an example, imagine you are:

1. A great shooter with no positive impact on other players. Your pay is high.

2. A great shooter with a negative impact on your team. Your pay is still high.

3. An okay shooter with a very positive impact on your team. Your pay is low.

The researchers found that adding a player with high spillover or a multiplier effect caused teammates to enjoy a 63 percent increase in results, but they would still only get paid for being an okay shooter.

You might read this and think, Why don't we just build a team of low-cost multipliers and win championships? And here is the other insight the researchers made: You get the value from these players when you have something big (as in big talent) to multiply. The magic happens when you have a balance of high-scoring talent and these glue players. Having a multiplier effect is only useful when you have something to multiply. A team made up of mediocre players will likely fail. Don't get me wrong: a team of all Shane Battiers might be the most loving and supportive team, which is good, but they would be fantastic at supporting each other through failure and loss . . . because, odds are, they would lose every game. You need a diversity of skills to be effective. You need to ensure that the balance between these diverse skills and team members is right too.

And that's one of the challenges for leaders. It's easier to locate the stars, but it's harder to spot the glue players. There is no NBA trophy for "Best Glue Player" or Academy Award for "Best Actor in a Multiplier Role." Glue players are often invisible, which makes them harder to find. So, what characteristics should we be looking for?

Unfortunately, there isn't a ton of research on this topic, but certain characteristics show up when people describe them.

High Emotional Intelligence

Glue players tend to see the world through someone else's eyes, which means they can pick up on social cues better. Not only does a great glue player understand the rules, but their social sensitivity helps them figure out the *unwritten* ones. We have all probably found ourselves in a situation where we did everything the way it was supposed to be done, but somehow our boss was upset. What we missed was that companies and teams have unwritten rules, everything from when to deliver bad news to how the boss likes to run a meeting to not listening to music so loudly on headphones that everyone around you can hear it (we get it, you're a millennial, you like Blink 182!). Overstepping these unspoken expectations could cost someone their job. A glue player mentally maps the rules so that it is easier for them to coordinate work and avoid landmines.

Having high social sensitivity often isn't enough on its own. You still need to be competent enough to do the work. Otherwise you're just an incompetent person who can empathize deeply with your boss as they're firing you. Shane was an exceptional athlete, but he is best paired with star talent. If a person doesn't have the skills needed to play the game, it doesn't matter how much glue they provide; they will never make it onto the court. After all, glue is only useful when it's sticking things together. When it's stuck on your fingers, suddenly glue is the most insufferable thing ever and should be banned by The Hague.

This means we need to find people who are skilled or competent and have high emotional intelligence. If you are going to build a team, don't be afraid to test people during the interview process on one of the many emotional intelligence tests available, so you can make sure that you have a good balance of skills on the team.

Benevolent/Team Orientation

Glue players also have a habit of putting the team above themselves. This might mean setting aside personal status so the team can shine, or it might mean sacrificing playing time because someone else is better suited to get a job done. When a team member consistently shows they are selfless and cares about the team, people trust them. Glue players don't trade on status; instead they lean on their emotional intelligence to build working relationships with everyone and turn the spotlight on others' contributions. As the name implies, glue players are often the connectors and confidants in the group. They're like that one kid in high school who's somehow friends with the jocks and the band geeks and the mathletes and the teachers. We all knew one, and though you probably didn't realize it at the time, the entire fabric of the school's social order depended on them. It's the same at any workplace. Look for the connectors, the ones who often gather people, make introductions, or are the ones people go to for advice.

Proactive Thinker

Since glue players put the team above themselves and understand the social structures of the organization, they are able to see beyond what is asked for, and instead do what is needed. If Shane just did his job, he would just practice every day and play his heart out, but he wouldn't talk to his teammates constantly on the court, he wouldn't read and memorize the shooting stats of the players from the opposing team, and he wouldn't ask the coach to bench him. Notice that they don't have to be in the formal leadership position; they lead from the back.

They might jump in when needed, and not because of their desire for attention or control, but rather because they know their strengths and do what is needed.

What are some examples of how glue players make things stick? They might take the time to give thoughtful feedback on your project or brew a new pot of coffee after they drink the last cup (an act of heroism second only to the Miracle on the Hudson). They might spend their weekend rewriting training manuals. They consistently do things that aren't required, assigned, or even asked for—but are desperately needed to help a team cohere and succeed.

I hope I've convinced you that glue players are special, but I also want to remind you that they are not a cure-all that helps an ailing team or organization. No doubt other kinds of skills—beyond emotional intelligence, benevolence, and proactive thinking—are doing their magic to create a successful team. Are there other skill sets that are important? Yes, without a doubt. But if you are going to build a team, you need to look past creating a star roster and also create a connected roster, by adding glue players.

We have learned what makes a super team and what to avoid, so now we want to understand how we fit in the bigger company and what we need to be aware of for the future of work.

Ideas in Action

When building a team, there are a few key ideas to consider:

- It is not about avoiding star talent, but making sure there is a balance of talent.

- Who can help this balance? Find your glue players or multipliers. These are the people who have high emotional intelligence, proactive thinking, and benevolent/team orientation.

What can you do:

- *The Dark Tetrad:* If you find yourself in a situation where you are dealing with someone who demonstrates some or all of the Dark Tetrad, the one and only takeaway is . . . you. You need to protect yourself in whatever ways you can, which I have outlined. Remember, your first responsibility is your safety. This includes your emotional well-being, family, career, and finances.

- *Know what you are hiring for:* Before you add people to the team, catalog the skills and resources of your current team members so that when you are adding new people, you can supplement with new resources.

- *Test for emotional intelligence:* When interviewing, speak to former employers and coworkers to see if potential candidates are glue players.

- *Give status to glue:* Create awards and recognition for the people who support the stars. For example, for most supportive player, allow people to submit who has helped them the most, and recognize those people. At companies where there are MVPs it is good to ask them who contributed the most but didn't get recognition.

- *To build trust:* Play some of the games available for free at www.JonLevy.com or read *You're Invited*.

Part III

Organizations—Unleashed

Chapter 10

Welcome to the Corporate Family

If we want to unleash the intelligence of your entire organization, let's start with a basic question: Why do companies exist?

- Do they function to make sure that their employees are cared for, since without the latter there wouldn't be any products or services?

- Are they responsible for being stewards of the planet, since we can't survive without it?

- Do they exist for the customers, since if you don't care about them, where will the money come from?

- Should a company focus purely on its investors/shareholders since they put the money in, took the risk, and expect to be compensated?

If you answered yes to all these questions, then you're obviously aware of the paradox at the heart of the modern company. For much of modern history, companies have struggled with these competing responsibilities, trying to determine which one is most important. But in 1970, famed economist and future Nobel Prize recipient Milton Friedman published an op-ed in the *New York Times* that changed the direction of business. He believed that companies had no social responsibility to society or the public and that the *only* responsibility of a company is to increase shareholder value. To quote Friedman, "there is one and only one social responsibility of business—to use its resources and engage in activities designed to increase its profits." Essentially, he argued, the leadership of a company must do anything in their power to increase the stock value no matter the impact on its people, products, customers, and the planet. At face value that could sound reasonable. If I take the risk of investing in a company and own it, the leadership should be a good steward and ensure that I make a profit. But in the decades since Friedman's proclamation, we've witnessed too many companies doing whatever they can to grow their stock value and ensure quarterly returns at the expense of their employees, their customers, and the planet—from Enron committing criminal offenses to Volkswagen faking emission standards in their cars to banks helping terrorist groups and opening fake accounts in people's names. If only Milton Friedman would write an op-ed justifying *my* worst impulses: "Why Jon Should Play Videogames to 2 a.m."

Or consider airplane manufacturer Boeing. The company was founded in 1916, and for most of its history it was a shining example of an open culture, led by engineers and focused on safety. It was so trusted that pilots used to say, "If it ain't Boeing, I ain't going."

In 1996, Boeing announced that it would be merging with McDonnell Douglas, an aerospace manufacturer known for its military planes. The merger would make Boeing the largest aircraft manufacturer in the world. There were a lot of concerns with McDonnell Douglas's attitude on engineering after issues with just one of their planes, the DC-10, led to more than 1,100 fatalities and the plane was grounded by the Federal Aviation Administration. Boeing's merger with McDonnell Douglas was like watching your best friend fall in love with someone who takes their socks off on flights: you know this is going to end terribly but they just won't listen, so you just have to sit back and watch it unfold. For some reason, even though Boeing was bigger and more successful, the cutthroat, profit-driven culture of McDonnell Douglas took control.

A year after the merger, the company announced a stock buyback program where the company's cash would be spent to pump up the stock price. A few years later, realizing how much the "engineering first" culture was distracting executives from the importance of growing the stock, company leadership moved the headquarters from the engineering and manufacturing center in Seattle to Chicago, which is two thousand miles away. As Boeing's then-CEO Phil Condit explained, "When the headquarters is located in proximity to a principal business . . . the corporate center is inevitably drawn into day-to-day business operations." If that sounds like "nonsensical corporate gobbledygook," that's because it is. Fortunately, I'm fluent in NCG, so let me translate. They literally said they don't want to be pestered by the difficulty of connecting with employees and understanding the challenges involved in designing and making a safe and innovative product, because that would just get in the way of the important work of increasing company stock value.

A few years later, Jim McNerney joined the company as CEO, and he was also committed to growing shareholder value. What was his plan? You start by slashing budgets, and then you give more dividends and do a stock buyback. From there his plan becomes more cringey. He developed a derogatory term for people who didn't care enough about company stock value and cared too much about a plane's integrity. He called them "phenomenally talented a**holes," and made it acceptable for his deputies to bully these engineers so that they would leave the company. The ones who remained weren't allowed to work on the new plane being designed, the Boeing Dreamliner. Instead McNerney cut the design budget to less than half of what it cost to develop the last plane. He saved money by outsourcing the work to contractors so he wouldn't need to deal with unions.

Yes, you read that right. Even though Boeing had some of the most talented engineers in the world, they outsourced the design of the world's most advanced flying machine, one with 2.3 million parts, to companies with no engineering departments. That would be like your hospital hiring a five-year-old as head of surgery. This is a product that needs a zero-failure policy.

It would take another three years for the plane to be released at a cost of $25 billion over budget. Then when flights began, problems sprung up, including two fires caused by defective batteries. In response, the FAA grounded all the new Dreamliners; it was the first time they had grounded a plane since the DC-10. Not bad for a product sold at about $225 million per.

During this fiasco, employees raised concerns and shared issues, but the leadership didn't listen, and why would they? They were now thousands of miles away, and these pesky complaints were just a distraction from the importance of increasing stock value. When journalists managed to get hidden-camera interviews with employees, most said they would never fly on the Dreamliner, knowing how it was built. A once-proud culture of engineers and assembly people were now scared of the product they were making.

But don't worry over Boeing, because the leadership had a new plan. Rather than using the company's money to make a great product, from 2014 to 2019 Boeing diverted 92 percent of its operating cash flow to dividends and share buybacks to benefit investors. Since 1998, share buybacks have consumed $70 billion. To the leadership's credit, they managed to increase stock value to $253 billion in 2018. When Boeing released their next plane, the 737-Max, they faced the same types of problems. Employees were ignored, corners were cut, and technical problems kept emerging. To make matters worse, their competitor Airbus had launched a popular, more fuel-efficient update to their flagship plane. So Boeing did what they had learned to do: they put huge pressure on their teams and incentivized them to push out a solution. Without getting into details, the 737-Max had much larger engines, and because of the way they were placed on the plane, if pilots tried to compensate and tilt the craft, they could cause it to crash. To account for this, Boeing installed a system to auto-level the plane, called MCAS, but the company never told the FAA or pilots because leadership was concerned that making too many changes would have the agency view it as a new plane that would require new pilot training, and then airlines wouldn't want to buy it.

Because of Boeing's negligence, in 2018 an Indonesian Airlines flight disappeared from radar soon after takeoff. We would later find out that because of a flaw in the 737-Max, it crashed, killing 189 people. The exact cause? MCAS relied on a sensor that could be blocked by something as silly as a floating balloon or bird—you know, those other things in the sky besides planes—and as a result, the plane would dive down to the ground or water. Boeing promised a fix within six weeks, but in that time, all they accomplished was another stock buyback at $20 billion. After all, according to Milton Friedman, their only responsibility was shareholder value. So how does this story end? Not well. Four months later there was still no fix, and even though pilots knew about MCAS, it led to another tragedy when an Ethiopian Airlines flight crashed. Finally, after a total of 346 people died, the FAA grounded the 737-Max until it could be proven safe to fly.

But that wasn't the end of problems for Boeing. In 2023 an Alaska Airlines flight from Portland, Oregon, to Ontario, California, suddenly depressurized when the door plug flew off midflight. If the passengers sitting next to it didn't have their seat belts on, they would have been blown out. The problem was that Boeing hadn't put in the bolts needed to keep it in place. On further investigation across the fleet, they found that similar shoddy work was done on other planes. The FAA discovered that Boeing employees feared retaliation for raising safety-related concerns, didn't believe changes would be made if they did report them, and didn't understand their role in the safety processes. Yeah, of course they felt that way; every signal from leadership told them to get the work done by any means necessary or else the company would lose money, and then they would lose their job.

In 2024, to avoid going to trial for the 737-Max crashes, Boeing pleaded guilty to felony charges. As a by-product of US law, felons are not allowed to do business with the US government, putting all of their military and NASA contracts at risk.

So how is Boeing's shareholder value doing? At the time of writing, the company is worth less than half of what it was at its peak. It spent almost all of its operating budget to pump up stock value that then disappeared because it didn't care about employees, customers, product, or its social responsibility. It is now a felon with a questionable future. They have lost employee, customer, and public trust and put the future of aviation at risk.

But even after all these problems, there is hope. When you speak to the employees of Boeing, you can hear their passion for creating great feats of innovation that improve people's lives and experiences. Executives with twenty, thirty, or more years of experience who have always fought the good fight for safety and quality are still there. That engineering spirit that made the company great may have been suppressed over the last years, but it is still alive, and in July 2024, Kelly Ortberg, former CEO of aerospace company Rockwell Collins and, most importantly, an engineer at heart, took over as CEO of Boeing. For the first time in decades, there is someone piloting Boeing through the inevitable turbulence who understands the product, the customer, and the challenges. Will Boeing make it through this? I don't know if we have a choice. Frankly, the world needs Boeing, and it will fall on Ortberg and his team to build trust back up with their workforce, customers, and those who fly.

Boeing's story shows us why shareholder value has been called "the error at the heart of corporate leadership." When you look at the research comparing similar-sized public companies focused on quarterly shareholder versus private companies focused on long-term growth, there was a clear winning strategy, and it wasn't focusing on stock value.

I find it amazing that I'm about to quote Jack Welch, famed CEO of GE from 1981 to 2001, the breeder of corporate super chickens, but even he understood the stupidity of shareholder value. He said that shareholder value is "the dumbest idea in the world. Shareholder value is a result, not a strategy . . . your main constituencies are your employees, your customers, and your products. Managers and investors should not set share price increases as their overarching goal. . . .

Short-term profits should be allied with an increase in the long-term value of a company."

In other words, the stock of a company increases over the long term because companies focus and invest in employees, customers, and products. It is the result of managing the complexities between these priorities that causes a company to be valuable. When you have great people, who feel respected and are treated well, they can make a fantastic product that customers love and pay for. That's what makes a company valuable and makes the stock go up.

So how do we balance a company's responsibilities when the answers to the questions I posed at the beginning of this chapter are yes, yes, yes, and yes? A company is responsible for caring for all of its stakeholders, including employees, customers, the world, and, yes, shareholders. When there are so many priorities, what tells employees how to treat each other, how to make decisions, and what defines the way they work? The answer is not simply in telling them how or training them. If you were to visit Boeing, I suspect you'd find piles of binders outlining proper procedure for product safety, but that didn't help because the signals that employees kept getting from leadership were that money reigns supreme.

Culture is the collection of attitudes, norms, traditions, behaviors, and beliefs shared in your organization, and the written and unwritten rules that people follow. The unwritten rules are communicated through status signals, catchphrases, or seeing people's actions. Imagine you come into Boeing on your first day and see a pile of damaged parts marked with red paint. Someone comes by, picks one up, rubs the paint off, and installs it on the plane. Can't imagine it? Unfortunately, you don't need to, because it happened. Seeing this, you are learning a collection of unwritten rules about how things operate at Boeing—what's okay to do or not do.

When people hear the word *culture*, they sometimes think it is about wasting money on frivolous Foosball tables and employee swag. If that's what you want to spend your budget on, you are welcome to, but I'm talking about defining how we interact and make decisions.

When people understand company culture, they don't need as much guidance for what decisions to make. Instead they are clear on what the organization prioritizes and values and they act consistent with that.

As a leader and team member, the idea of affecting the company culture may feel overwhelming, especially if you are part of a large multinational company, with tens or hundreds of thousands of employees. It may not be your job to transform an entire company, but understanding what defines culture—and shaping it—will have an impact on the team or teams you work with directly. So, what about all that talk about companies being one big happy family? All too often, it's cheap talk meant to hide the reality that companies, unlike families, fire people when quarterly earnings are a little off. Instead, a company is more like a sports team. We understand that the team's responsibility is to have the highest intelligence so that it can keep winning according to the rules of the game. This means people will be recruited, while others will retire or be cut, but the team will continue. In the same way, at a company, people may come and go, but while someone is on the team, the company wants them to perform at their best so that they deliver a fantastic product to customers and hopefully take care of the planet at the same time. It's not always realistic to keep everyone on the team, and that's okay. Frankly, it is healthy to give people an opportunity to grow at different organizations and make room for new talent with new ideas.

What's important is that when someone is on the team, they work in an effective culture and feel like they are part of it. So, let's explore the different aspects of culture and how they work to increase your team's intelligence and the organization's collective genius as a whole. A strong culture has four aspects:

1. Membership

2. Influence

3. Integration and fulfillment of needs

4. Shared history and values

Membership

That feeling that you belong and are part of the group is an incredible driver for people. We explored how psychological safety was not only critical for the second pillar of team intelligence—attention—but was also a predictor of effective teams. To create that sense of membership, people need boundaries, emotional safety, belonging, personal investment, and a common symbol system.

Membership: Boundaries

There is a clear line between who is on the inside and outside. There are many ways companies do this. Zappos is famous for offering people thousands of dollars to quit after their training period. If someone accepts, they are saying it is clearly not the right cultural fit. Those who stay are now more aligned with the company, its values, and its mission. Remember that for team intelligence to be high, we need alignment so we can reason well. Anyone who is on the inside is now committed to that journey.

Meanwhile, on your first day working at Walt Disney World, Mickey Mouse, the most iconic of their characters, takes time from greeting families to welcome new employees. This might not seem like a big deal, but at Disney everyone wants to see Mickey, and this shows employees that they are on the inside, that they are so important that the company's most important asset came to them to welcome them. They are valued.

How do you signal that people are now on the inside of a culture? Do they need to go through a process? Is there a celebration or a welcome announcement? Do they receive a pin or status marker? Or is it just an HR meeting about benefits? It doesn't need to be a crazy party, but having a tradition on the team level can go a long way.

Membership: Emotional Safety

As I mentioned in Chapter 7, LEGO's tradition of a campfire conversation is a mechanism for increasing emotional safety. It allows employees to voice any concerns and be heard without feedback. As a result, issues are out in the open and can be handled. When the biggest safety issue employees have to worry about is accidentally stepping on a LEGO block in their bare feet, you've got a pretty safe company culture. Traditions like these demonstrate to employees that the company trusts and values them.

What traditions or habits can you put in place either for your team or the organization? Some of my favorites include:

- *Asking at a meeting:* Ask "What am I missing here?" "Help me see where I might be wrong." or "Can someone be a devil's advocate?"

- *Rewarding spotting a problem:* 20/20 is great vision, 20/10 is even better. Give people a 20/10 award for finding a problem before it comes up and having the courage to mention it.

- *Designating a counterpoint:* Pick one person at every meeting to find the weaknesses in the ideas so the holes can be patched before the idea goes live. Nothing worse than shipping a solution only to see it sink.

Membership: A Sense of Belonging and Identification

People from Amazon are Amazonians, Google employees are Googlers, and if they leave, they are Xooglers. If a company only cares about profits and treats its employees badly, employees won't feel a sense of belonging strong enough to identify as part of the team. Instead they will identify as chopped liver, or small fry, or any number of unsavory monickers that sound like they're from the 1940s. In an online forum, an Uber employee said, "Our founding CEO called us Boobers. Our current CEO calls us entitled." You can get a sense of the culture that was created early on in the company. It is no surprise that there were so many issues.

Does your organization or team have a name for its members? If not, come up with a few and see if any stick. We jokingly used to call our dinner alumni Burrito Makers, because that's what we cook at the dinners, but thankfully it didn't stick. This is even something you can use with your team. Self-identification is an important part of team membership. And you will know things are bad when employees distance themselves from the company like it is an embarrassing relative at Thanksgiving dinner.

Membership: Personal Investment

Remember the Ikea effect, that people care more about the things they invest effort into. If we want people to care about the culture, give them opportunities to invest effort. This may be hosting gatherings and workshops, providing input on company policies and strategy, doing volunteer work together, and seeing the way their contributions have a larger positive impact. Personal investment goes beyond the work itself; it also means supporting coworkers and feeling comfortable to ask for that support. Unless employees invest effort into one another through their personal and professional relationships, we can't expect them to be connected enough to feel like they are part of a culture. Ultimately culture shows up in the interactions between people; we observe, repeat, and often add our own twist. But that kind of cultural contagion can only happen when companies provide employees with opportunities to connect with each other.

No, I'm not talking happy hours. I'm not sure why companies keep thinking the solution to connecting people is having them awkwardly stand around each other while drinking alcohol. At famed sock company Bombas, CEO David Heath takes the entire company to summer camp for a few days every year, just to bond. The objective isn't to define the sales goals, but to ensure that people feel connected enough to do the work. He and his amazing team accomplish this through fun activities, games, and conversations.

For Bombas this makes perfect sense. Their core values include fun and collaboration. Do you need to replicate this? Of course not. It might not be realistic or even consistent with your company culture, but it serves as a fantastic example. The question you need to ask yourself is, "How are people feeling personally invested, not just professionally?"

Membership: A Common Symbol System

Symbols go beyond the insane number of stickers some people have on their laptops and extend to the catchphrases, outfits, and language you use. Strong cultures often have inside jokes, stories, or sayings that outsiders don't understand or know to look for. In a healthy culture, those symbols align with the company's values. I mentioned one, "If it ain't Boeing, I ain't going," because it refers to the high commitment to quality they used to have.

A great example of this was John Legere, the former CEO of T-Mobile. If you look at old photos of him, you have never seen a person more fitting of the title of "a corporate suit." But when he took over as the leader of T-Mobile, he needed to bring the culture of the "Un-Carrier" to life. He grew out his hair to his shoulders and switched his suit for a T-Mobile magenta T-shirt with leather jacket. Ever heard of Guns N' Roses? Well, John looked like the Slash of cellular phones. If that doesn't scream to the industry, "We aren't like you!" I don't know what does. To this day T-Mobile is still seen as the rebel in the phone industry. Part of that is having clear symbols that align with their values. If you go to a meeting at T-Mobile, they ask themselves, is this what an Un-Carrier would do? You would never hear that at AT&T or Verizon, because they have different cultures.

But you can also see that having that phrase helps people make decisions faster. They could ask, "Is this ad, promotion, product, etc. consistent with an Un-Carrier?" If not, find something else. But notice that since it is part of the culture, that phrase is repeated constantly and so it accelerates the decision-making process countless times a day. Having a strong culture creates shortcuts that save the company money in the long run.

In Southwest Airlines' heyday, every employee knew its purpose: "To connect people to what's important in their lives through friendly, reliable, and low-cost air travel." Being the "friendly, reliable, and low-cost" carrier was repeated so often, employees knew how to make better decisions; it was part of their culture. You want to sing "Happy Birthday" to a customer? Is it friendly, and will it negatively impact reliability and cost? Since it is consistent with those values, you can see countless very sweet videos online of people being sung to by the crew. But what if you want to throw confetti? That might be friendly, but it would affect reliability and cost. It would mean the cleanup crew has to work longer, which would delay the plane boarding. And so the answer is no. Notice that an employee doesn't need to ask, because the culture is to be "friendly, reliable, and low-cost." If it meets those standards they can make a quick decision.

What do people repeat at your work, and is it something you really want them to be saying? Does it align with the company's values or decent behavior? If not, interrupt it and start new phrases, create new symbols, and even give out new swag. I call this the "pumpkin-spicification process": if you insist something is important, like pumpkin spice flavoring, eventually it becomes a cultural trend and everyone from salsa makers to avocado oil producers (yes, really) will jump on the bandwagon. Whatever you think is important, repeat it so often that other people start saying it, or they make fun of you for saying it so much, because that's how we know it is getting into the culture.

Influence

Notice that Boeing culture went from listening to people and valuing their expertise to employees being ignored and scared to speak up. When people feel like they don't matter, it has a profound impact on their desire to work. They disengage because their efforts are meaningless. If you want your employees to create a great product and put in extra effort, they need to feel that they have influence, and are being influenced by their environment.

Are people at the company invited to suggest improvements? Are those suggestions listened to, and responded to? Do they feel empowered to take action to fix issues? Maybe their influence is found in another way. Can people easily start employee resource groups, gather coworkers, or run a training?

It isn't realistic for everyone to have influence at every level, but it is realistic for people to feel like they matter to their team.

Integration and Fulfillment of Needs

A healthy culture tells people: This is where we are going. If you are up for that journey, you should join us, but if you aren't, you should find an organization that is a better match for what you want. We're talking about our old friend alignment. It isn't about attracting the most talent; it's about getting the people you need for the journey you are going on. One wild example of this is that while gentle denominations of religious groups have been on the decline for generations, strict denominations of Christianity, Judaism, and Islam have been growing. These groups are unapologetic about where they are going, and there is a certain clarity and structure that strict cultures provide that strengthens them. I am not saying you need to create a strict culture; that would be pointless if it doesn't align with your values. What I'm saying is to let people know what you are about, where you are going, and what their opportunity is to be part of that.

If it isn't clear where the organization is going and how people fit into that, you will face a lot of challenges.

I should point out that often with new leadership or business changes, the company's direction can change. Researchers examining over 10 million internal communications at a midsize company found that employees who had a high cultural fit in terms of language and communication styles had more frequent raises and promotions, but what was a greater predictor of success was cultural adaptability. As said by the researchers, "Employees who could quickly adapt to cultural norms as they changed over time were more successful than employees who exhibited high cultural fit when first hired." The first kind of employees are dinosaurs, the second kind are sharks. Both very old and very cool, but I only still worry about one when I'm at the beach.

As you are looking to add people to the team, it is inevitable that you'll face change. Instead of looking just at fit, also look for adaptability.

Shared History and Values

This may be the most definitive characteristic of culture, because everything else stems from it. Sometimes a group mythology or shared history is made up, and oddly that can be okay. The people who work at Marvel don't think the comic book characters are real, any more than the good people at Red Bull believe they've conquered gravity, but their values and stories can still set an example.

A story that apparently is true, but is often told wrong, is that about forty years ago in Fairbanks, Alaska, a man walked into a Nordstrom luxury department store while rolling a tire alongside and asked for a refund. As you can imagine, the store associate who greeted the customer, Craig Trounce, was incredibly confused. Imagine walking into an Apple Store and asking for a refund on a sandwich. Craig had heard that in 1975, Nordstrom had bought a few companies that offered an eclectic collection of goods, so it was somehow possible there was a tire among them, perhaps alongside other seventies offerings like a Nixon campaign button or the Coca-Cola hot dog toaster (boy, the seventies were weird). More importantly, Nordstrom has an incredible commitment to caring for its customers. So Craig did the only thing appropriate: he called around, found a fair price, and gave the man who had traveled fifty miles to return the tire a full refund on a product the company probably didn't sell. To this day, Nordstrom shares this story with employees to exemplify how they want their customers treated and how to make decisions. According to the company, "[T]he tire story has become so important to our culture, we even hang tires in some of our stores and break rooms as a reminder of our commitment to our customers."

The mythology and stories we share and repeat teach us important lessons about who the company is and how to make decisions. I have worked with companies who sourced stories from employees that exemplify their values or how to handle a situation. They share and reshare them at important times such as onboarding, training, or when they reach an important junction. You can ask yourself, what behavior are you trying to elevate or give status to? Then search for those stories in your organization and tell them and retell them until they become your company mythology.

When Todd Kahn took over as the CEO of the American fashion house Coach, he knew that a command-and-control model wouldn't work for him or the brand. He realized that if you are going to be a dominant leader you need to be right every time, because no one will tell you when you are wrong. He had experienced that model and saw firsthand the terrible consequences. Since it's impossible to always be right, he needed to find a way to have employees at every level of the company understand their role and how to use their own judgment based on the values of the organization. So they developed the COACH Ways of Working:

- **Common sense:** When you are making a work choice, be reasonable and use common sense. If you think something doesn't make sense, don't do it. If you are sitting in a meeting and think, Wow, I would *never* spend my money in this way, you have to speak up and say something.

- **Opt out:** If it doesn't make sense for you to be in a meeting, opt out so you can do real work. If something is a time suck and isn't critical to the work, opt out. Clearly, this doesn't mean cutting corners; it means don't waste time on things that aren't needed.

- **Accept imperfection:** This isn't referring to the product; that needs to meet the highest standards. The imperfection is in information and sharing. In life you will never have perfect information, so you have to make decisions based on the information you have at the time. The team won't punish or blame people for making thoughtful decisions even if they are imperfect. Adopting a "test and learn" culture that moves quickly and iterates will always do better than one trying to accomplish the impossible task of addressing all the risks.

- **Courageous:** Take action and do not operate out of fear. The company will support you if things don't turn out the way you had hoped. People are expected to learn from their mistakes, so they don't repeat them.

- **Have fun!:** Creating beautiful things that people love should be a joyous experience. That's why most of us joined this industry!

In the years since Todd took over Coach, the brand has grown to over $5 billion in annual revenue, at the highest absolute profitability in the history of the brand, and you can see why. He creates a culture where employees are given a clear set of ways of working and trusted to make their own decisions. He has codified what it means to work at Coach and made it simple to remember. He knew he was on to something when he walked into a store and, on their own, they created stickers with the COACH Ways of Working.

As you look at your culture, ask yourself, is it supporting and creating a connected team or organization that can unlock its collective genius? Or is the culture destroying trust and competence the way Boeing did? No culture is perfect, and it isn't stagnant either. Culture evolves and grows with the times, business pressures, leadership, and political changes.

Adapting to Change

It takes a long time for us to adapt to a cultural or technological change. We need to develop new norms, cultural etiquette, and technology to compensate. When Covid-19 shut down many offices, the sudden disruption created new ways of working that we are still trying to figure out, and with artificial intelligence (AI) playing a greater role in our work and personal lives, our cultures and our team intelligence will inevitably be tested.

Postpandemic, with many workers still working remotely at least part of the time, with teams distributed around the world, culture has moved from the office to the level of team or manager. The truth is, managers were never hired to be cultural ambassadors or camp counselors. They were hired because they were great at ad sales, programming, accounting, or some other specialized skill. That's like asking the baker of your kid's birthday cake to also be a magician.

To make the situation more complex, the way we tend to build trust is through familiarity, shared effort, vulnerability, and common ground, but we haven't developed new habits for this on virtual platforms. When we gather in person, conversations naturally open up, we learn about each other's families, we walk together after a meeting, and if someone drops some papers, a coworker helps pick them up. Vulnerability loops open and close much faster. So, what did we learn about compensating for this when teams are distributed?

Although it feels frivolous to some, people need time to get to know one another. We want to connect our teams the way Eisenhower connected the US. Without it we often don't have the trust needed to get work done. The Swedes have a tradition called Fika. No, it's not Ikea's latest sofa. It's where employees take a break to share coffee and treats with friends, and it is very intentional. They might even Fika while sitting on a Finnala (which, yes, is an Ikea sofa). When MIT professor Alex Pentland wanted to help call-center employees be more effective, he suggested they synchronize coffee breaks. This would allow people to connect, talk to each other, bond, share knowledge, and emotionally regulate. Low-performing employees increased their effectiveness by 20 percent, and for many employees, satisfaction went up 10 percent. That one change led to an estimated $15 million profit for the company. Not bad for a little intentionality in creating a Fika and helping people bond.

As distance increases, so does our need to be intentional about the way we communicate and connect. Because we aren't around each other, simply timing breaks won't cut it. We also can't depend on managers to come up with solutions, since they are already overworked and will default to virtual happy hours where the extroverts get drunk and talk over everyone. Our people deserve something better than Karl from Sales practicing his open mic set at 4:30 p.m. on a Friday Zoom.

So, my team and I developed a series of experiments to see if we can provide simple solutions that have a long-term impact. The constraints were simple. Any solution needed to be:

- *Fast:* If it took too long to run, no one would do it.

- *Turnkey:* It didn't need any training and could be run out of the box.

- *Scalable:* It needed to work as easily for 200,000 people as 200. Otherwise, it is useless for large organizations.

- *Inexpensive:* If every time you ran it, it required hiring someone, it wouldn't be cost-effective.

- *Upskilled:* Companies kept telling me that no one wanted another passive video training program. If these activities could teach employees a concept or lesson, it would go from being seen by some as frivolous to essential.

- *Culturally relevant:* Ideally any lessons should align with and reinforce the company's values.

The solution became *Turnkey Teams*, a collection of scripted activities that any manager or team member could run on topics ranging from communication and creativity to trust and decision-making. Each activity bonded teams both in person and remotely while having fun and learning. With options that are 15, 30, or 60 minutes to choose from they were ideal for anything from a team meeting to an off-site.

We tested these solutions with one of the four major US airlines and one of the largest banks in the country. The results were fantastic. Notice how much more intentional we had to be as the distance grew. We had to design twenty to thirty of these activities for companies so that it matched their culture, and so that managers would actually use them. They had to be packaged with all relevant information, and we even created invitation emails so that the team would know what they had to prepare ahead of time. Companies can now have monthly cultural moments happening at every level of the organization, and there is quality control in the design to make sure it is consistent. Instead of culture being an office experience, it is a team experience. (To support you and your team, we created some free games and activities that you can run. They can be found on my website, www.JonLevy.com.) By finding opportunities to run these kinds of activities, teams can bond and build the trust necessary to unlock their intelligence.

Putting It All Together

Across the three sections of the book—Leadership, Teams, Organizations—we covered a lot of topics, but as a leader and team member, how do they all fit together?

- *Leadership:* At its core, leadership is defined by having followers, and people follow because you have super skills that are so strong that when people engage with them, they feel there will be a new and better future. There are no specific essential skills for leadership, but there are clear best practices that separate leaders from effective leaders. Specifically, that effective leader makes sure that the team is connected and has enough trust to accomplish its goal. As a leader you don't have to be the person on the team that creates these conditions, but you are responsible to make sure you pick the right person to do it and that it happens. Ultimately, this sets the condition for maximizing team intelligence.

- *Team intelligence:* Although having competent people is essential, adding star talent to a team won't make it smarter, unless the team's dynamics, habits, and makeup are in place. Although the leader doesn't need to be the person who brings these habits to the group, it is the leader's role to make sure they are being adopted. The three key areas are:
    - *Reasoning:* For a team to get from where they are to where they want to be, they need to be aligned. We need to move away from a super-chicken mentality,

where people are self-serving. Remember, the only metric of an effective basketball coach is that team members pass more when that coach takes over. That is because they have moved from being self-serving to working together as a team toward a common goal. To unlock the team's intelligence, everyone needs to know the organizational goals and understand how the team's goals support that, how their individual role supports the team, and, ideally, how their personal goals align with their work. When everything is going in the same direction, we can reason.

- *Attention:* A team succeeds when it knows what to focus on, when, and how. They synchronize their work, allowing for bursty communication, conversational turn-taking, and high psychological safety. This means that when they meet, they come to conclusions and clear next steps, and then they go their separate ways and work uninterrupted. What helps these dynamics is having team members with high emotional intelligence. They allow for communication to flow more effectively and defuse potential problems.

- *Resources:* Put simply, teams with more diverse resources (skills, knowledge, life experience, mental models, contacts, etc.) outperform, but the key is in making the implicit explicit. People need to know what resources their teammates have and where to find resources in the company. It is important when hiring to consider the resources that people bring.

To unlock these key areas more effectively, find your glue players and empower them. These are the people who multiply other people's results. They often have very high emotional intelligence. They are team-oriented and are proactive thinkers.

- *Organization and culture:* The habits that unlock team intelligence are most effective when they are ingrained into the culture of your organization. Culture is the collection of attitudes, norms, traditions, behaviors, and beliefs shared in your organization, and the written and unwritten rules that people follow. To ingrain these habits so they become the norm of the organization, we rely on the four characteristics that define a team: membership, influence, integration and fulfillment of needs, and shared history and values. When this happens, your people will naturally embody these habits rather than have to constantly reinforce them.

As we look to apply these ideas and unlock the collective genius of our teams, I want you to see what this looks like in practice by sharing one of the wildest stories I have ever come across in my life. The story of how an ordinary person learned these lessons and by applying them made a profound impact. Prepare to meet a man I like to describe as a smart Forrest Gump, because he kept finding himself at the wrong place at the right time to change history.

Ideas in Action

- Culture is the collection of attitudes, norms, traditions, behaviors, and beliefs shared in your organization, and the written and unwritten rules that people follow.

- The unwritten rules are communicated through status signals, catchphrases, or seeing people's actions.

- You can have a profound impact on the culture of the teams you work with by focusing on these areas:
    - *Membership:* How do we signal that people are on the inside, how do we welcome people, what are your team symbols and catchphrases?
    - *Influence:* Do your teammates feel like they are heard and matter? It isn't about doing everything people suggest but that they feel that they have a voice.
    - *Integration and fulfillment of needs:* Are team members clear on where the organization is going? When there is alignment people are more committed to the outcome and are a better cultural fit.
    - *Shared history and values:* Are your people clear on your values? How have you simplified what the team is about and how to make decisions?

Chapter 11
Becoming the Leader We Need

It was like "Europe had come apart at the seams." People were dying at an alarming rate, and as an ambulance driver on his first day, Draper L. Kauffman was overwhelmed by the chaos. Reading this, you might think he was saving lives from the spread of the Covid-19 global pandemic but instead Kauffman, an American volunteer in France, was on the front line of an even larger threat, the Nazi forces making their way from Germany across the world. The date was May 10, 1940, and German soldiers had just invaded Belgium, Luxembourg, and the Netherlands, the three countries that provided a buffer between northern France and Germany.

Draper was terrified trying to maneuver his ambulance between explosions in order to get to the injured French soldiers. Even with his training as a US Naval Academy graduate, he was not prepared for the brutality of war. Fortunately, what he lacked in experience, he made up for with his desire to serve and learn.

After graduating from the Naval Academy and not getting a commission because of his bad eyesight, he volunteered as an ambulance driver in France. As documented by his letters home and stories from his family, it all began with Draper's first rescue. While mortars exploded around his ambulance, Draper maneuvered to pick up a casualty, a member of an elite special operations team known as the Corps Franc. Over the next weeks, as the casualties increased and Draper continued to risk his life to save them, he had earned their respect. When writing home, Draper shared, "You were either accepted by the Corps Franc or you weren't accepted, and the two were miles apart." If you were, "there wasn't anything they wouldn't do for you. . . . If one member of the patrol was attacked and there were five others, they would attack fifty Germans to save the man. . . ." As an American volunteer risking his life to support them, he had gained their trust and was invited into their inner circle.

This may be one of the most important lessons Draper would learn. The connections between team members allow them to function and thrive even in the most extreme conditions. When we face challenges and stress, knowing we are part of a team can mean the difference between crumbling from the pressure and having the support we need.

After months on the front line, Draper was reassigned to what was supposed to be the safety of the French countryside, but while picking up casualties, a German infantry captured him. He was now a prisoner of war, slowly wasting away behind barbed wire in a POW camp. Although conditions were better than in the concentration and work camps, he had fallen from a healthy 165 pounds to a mere 125.

In the most unexpected of events, one day a nun walked up to the camp entrance, demanding to see the Americans being held and for their release according to the Geneva Conventions. When the guard refused, she hit his helmet in the most badass move by a nun during World War II since Julie Andrews sang "The Sound of Music." Likely confused by the interaction, she was let in. The POWs quickly passed her any information they could as to send word to their worried families. Apparently the nun had caused a commotion at almost a dozen bases and managed, with the help of the US embassy, to have all the Americans freed on the fact that the US and Germany were not at war, and so Germany had no right to detain them. A short time later, Draper was a free man.

Here we see a second critical lesson: there is no set of noble skills that define leadership. The nun would have never been considered a traditional leader, especially not in a time of war. She didn't have the skills to confront Germany head-on. So how did she solve a problem like the Nazis? She leaned into her super skills. She was tenacious and unconventional, and because of that, she was able to get the US embassy's help, get past German security, and get those men free.

Draper's time as a POW only served to reinforce his conviction that Germany had to be stopped before the war reached American soil. With the US refusing to join the fight, and France under German siege, he enlisted in the British Royal Navy and was commissioned in its Volunteer Reserve. Being severely underweight after his imprisonment and having poor eyesight, he was sent to Officer Training School.

During his time there, bombings by German forces and air raid warnings had become a part of life for the students. One day an unexploded German bomb landed near the school's mess hall. Unsure what to do, students tiptoed around it on their way to class, but when they returned for dinner, the bomb had detonated, and the defusal team with it. The students were called for a meeting and were asked for six volunteers to join the army bomb disposal squad. If there was anything more stressful for a soldier than driving an ambulance through a war zone, it might be being in a POW camp, and if there was anything more stressful than that, it was being on the bomb disposal squad. He was collecting stressful military jobs like they were Pokémon. Draper grappled with the idea, having seen the risks firsthand, but realized that if he wanted to save lives, this was an honorable role.

Here we discover the next lesson. Effective teams are created not by super chickens stuck in the cult of self, but by creating a super team where people are selfless. We are capable of much more when we act in the service of a unified goal, when we are aligned on what we all need to accomplish, and how. You can already see that Draper had the classic characteristics of a glue player. Draper, the other volunteers, and in fact any person, team, or company acting with a greater purpose consistently accomplishes more than when we are purely self-serving. Let's be honest: no sane group of people would volunteer to work on bomb defusal after having seen the horror the explosions create unless there was something more important at stake than self-interest. And no sane basketball player asks to be benched like Shane Battier did, if they are only interested in personal glory. But in both cases, there was a more important mission. Draper wanted to save lives and to do his part in preventing the war from coming to the US, and so just as he embraced his fears as an ambulance driver, he would do so again to save the people of the United Kingdom as a bomb defuser.

The fears we face in our careers are very different from those Draper had to struggle with, unless your job is literally fighting the rise of fascism, in which case this story is less metaphor and more instruction manual. In our careers, it is not a fear of a bomb that we need to embrace, but fear of being vulnerable. What we learned is that vulnerability is the basis of trust. The first step in creating a meaningful connection with the team is signaling vulnerability. We fear that if we ask for help, we will look incompetent or be rejected. We fear that we will be taken advantage of, overlooked for a promotion, or worse, yelled at or punished by a toxic boss. What we need, just as Draper needed, is a greater purpose so we are willing to deal with our fear, and a group of people to face it with. Otherwise, if we have no connection to our coworkers or company and no greater vision to inspire us, and we are just sitting at home or in a cubicle working, then it will be appealing to jump to another job if offered slightly higher pay or a slightly shorter commute. Those teams that are more connected and have a greater vision will be the ones that thrive. It is the first pillar of intelligent teams: reasoning. For teams to reason they need alignment. People need to know where the organization is going, the team's role in the organization, their role within the team, and ideally, how their personal goals align with their work goals. Remember that the mark of an effective coach, leader, or manager is that their people are connected and are playing for a common goal. When everyone is headed in the same direction the team becomes smarter. Draper and the other volunteers were perfectly aligned with the mission to save the world.

As attacks progressed and Draper's experience as a defuser grew, he was recruited to the Mine Disposal Command. (Think all the dangers of bomb disposal, except now you can't even see the bombs. So way worse? Yes, way worse.) Here he had the privilege to report to Captain Currey. Currey was a leader who instilled complete confidence in his people and "paid no attention to bureaucracy." As you can imagine, trying to micromanage a bomb defuser from a distance is a very bad idea. Instead you need to have them feel safe enough to come to you when there is a problem and be available whenever they need you. Captain Currey made sure his officers "could get a hold of him on the phone at any hour of the day or night for advice, taking precedence over anyone else of whatever rank."

Currey's trust in his people and push against bureaucracy and rank allowed his team to unlock the second pillar of team intelligence: knowing what to pay attention to, and when. The skill needed for attention is synchronized bursty communication. Currey's team could come together, speak freely, share their insights and updates from what they were discovering in the field, define a strategy, and then go their separate ways to do their work uninterrupted. After all, again, trying to micromanage a bomb defuser is a recipe for disaster. Here we see another lesson that should be learned. Managers who succeed don't try to manage people but instead focus on managing outcomes. Here the KPIs were clear: Did the bomb go off and kill dozens of people? No? Great! Pizza party for the whole team! Captain Currey developed a high level of trust in his officers' competence and would leave them to do their work. Instead of micromanaging them, he was there to provide support and remove roadblocks day and night. One more time: If you try to micromanage a bomb defuser, things will go very bad. Instead you need to be available to them whenever they need you. Fundamentally, when you empower competent people, they are incentivized to make good choices. This level of trust in them breeds greater levels of trust in return. On the other hand, micromanaging breeds exhaustion and frustration, and reduces confidence. In a job where physical safety is at a minimum, psychological safety has to be at a premium.

After a year and a half in Europe as an ambulance driver, POW, and bomb/mine defuser, Draper was coming home to the States to visit his family for a month's leave, or at least that's what he thought. With growing tension between German forces and the US Navy, the US military needed to create a Bomb Disposal School. When word got out about Draper's expertise, he found himself in the odd situation of being transferred to the US military without his approval or even them talking to him. If sentimental 1980s–90s movies taught us anything, he would now take on his most terrifying and possibly gratifying job yet: teaching.

He was to create the Navy Bomb Disposal School, but on December 7, 1941, days before his first class, Japanese forces attacked Pearl Harbor in Hawaii, killing more than 2,400 people and officially bringing the US into World War II. During the attack, a 500-pound bomb was dropped outside the doors of Fort Schofield's ammunition depot, and Draper would be flown in to defuse it. It seemed that once again, no matter where Draper went, he would find himself in the middle of history. He was like a smart Forrest Gump with bad eyesight. On the bright side, this gave him the first material to use for training his students, and in time it also earned him a Navy Cross, one of the many decorations he was awarded.

Draper knew that his job was to ensure that graduates were competent under the most harrowing conditions. Experience had taught him that the biggest risk to their lives, besides the bomb itself, was fatigue and the carelessness it causes. To test these men, he devised a grueling final exam that demonstrated the seriousness of the work. It lasted between 25 and 29 hours straight and included extensive digging (much of bomb defusal is digging) and physical tasks.

Draper understood that this difficult training provided his graduates with a sense of competence and belonging. Those who passed would earn their place in a brotherhood and could feel confident they had been trained well. In that way, earning a spot on Draper's bomb defusal team was like being initiated into a fraternity, except that instead of fighting for their right to party, they were fighting for the freedom of the entire world.

With the school up and running, Draper was called in for a new highly secretive mission. German forces had installed obstacles across two thousand miles of France's beaches to prevent Allied forces from landing. His orders were to figure out how to demolish them, and there was no time to waste. Now Draper was responsible for creating an Underwater Demolitions School to destroy objects on a foreign beach he had never seen before.

Taking the best people from bomb defusal and adding diverse expertise from other teams, he assembled an initial group. Needing to weed out people who wouldn't be able to handle the danger, he took an eight-week joint Army-Navy reconnaissance training and condensed it into one week of grueling activities, night swims, long runs, hand-to-hand combat, and sleep and food deprivation. It was like many of us in college during finals week—trying to cram a semester's worth of material into a few days. Once prepared, Draper did something completely unprecedented: he realized that he couldn't expect his men to participate if he didn't do it himself, so he joined in. By the end, 40 percent of the class either quit or were injured. In the words of one of Draper's men, "the dirtiest, rottenest jobs that we tackle, he is there doing as well as the rest of us. How could you not respect him? You may be mad at him, but by God in a short time we all admired Draper Kauffman."

To make it through challenging situations, we need to have a profound level of trust. As we have discovered, trust is made of competence, honesty, and benevolence. Draper earned the respect and trust of his men because he demonstrated all three. It wasn't enough for them that he was knowledgeable and skilled (competent). By putting himself through that week of hell, he showed that he believed in the value of the training (honest) and that it was done in all of their best interests (benevolent). What made his participation so extraordinary was that at the time, officers such as Draper wouldn't train alongside their enlisted men, but Draper had seen the strength of the Corps Franc, the camaraderie and trust they needed under impossible situations, and so he put himself in the heart of it. Benevolence is at the core of every trusted relationship. If you don't feel that people have your best interests at heart, why would you interact with them, especially when your life is on the line? This trust and connection that he created in turn laid the groundwork for creating an intelligent team.

It also demonstrates another important idea. In the business world, we often train leadership separately from the team, but that doesn't necessarily help the team operate well together. Because Draper, his officers, and the enlisted men trained together, they could develop a common language and respect, and much like Captain Currey from the British bomb squad, Draper ensured his men could speak freely. Junior men could be candid and even share what may be a dissenting view, without the risk of being alienated from the group or punished. Rank was meaningless when it came to solving problems. What mattered was accomplishing the mission safely.

With the initial amphibious team's selection set, the Underwater Demolitions Team's mission was finally revealed to them. Their task was to clear the way for soldiers to take the beaches at Normandy, France, and Saipan, Japan, in what became known as D-Day. There was no playbook for something like this. Intel suggested that half a million obstacles had been erected across the roughly twelve hundred miles of beaches in Normandy alone. As Lieutenant Commander Kaj Larsen points out, "At high tide soldiers and ships would be stopped by barbed wire, sharpened spikes, cement triangles, and metallic objects that looked like oversized jacks; not to mention mines. All this had to be cleared while being shot at by enemy forces and snipers. As if this wasn't enough, they were operating for hours in frigid water in nothing but shorts; wet suits hadn't been invented yet."

With the stakes being so high, the UDT divers had no time to complain about limited information. They needed to act and adapt by testing strategies as quickly as possible. If the UDT divers didn't find what worked fast, thousands of fellow soldiers would drown, be shot, or get blown up. The group had full alignment about what they had to accomplish and what each person's role was on the team. They had the first pillar of team intelligence: reasoning. Even though they faced limited information and no experience, the psychological safety developed during selection and training allowed them to have synchronized communication habits like burstiness and equal conversation time, needed for good attention, the second pillar of team intelligence. That way all the team had to worry about was the bomb blowing up, and not their boss blowing up at them for asking a question or offering feedback. The UDT divers needed to find solutions quickly, so they took good ideas from wherever they could find them. Draper attributed many of the incredible innovations the UDT divers created not to experienced officers, but to junior officers or enlisted men. Their strength came from the fact that their team was composed of people with different expertise from across the military. This is the third and final pillar of team intelligence: resources. Teams with diverse resources like mental models, experience, education, contacts, etc. far outperform and can solve problems faster. The UDT divers succeeded not in spite of coming from different backgrounds, but because of them. With their diversity of knowledge and experience, they were able to innovate and develop strategies for demolishing and clearing the objects across the beaches. Not to spoil D-Day for those of you who haven't finished high school history, but his team did an amazing job.

In the days building up to and following D-Day, the UDT divers performed incredible feats of heroism, from setting underwater charges and blowing up obstacles to swimming miles while under fire to save lives. They cleared the way for soldiers, sailors, and marines, in the process suffering significant casualties, so that Allied forces could push back the German military and turn the tide to take back Europe. The UDT divers took on many of the most challenging missions in World War II and emerged as legends, with Draper personally leading a team in Saipan.

Two decades after the heroism the UDT divers demonstrated in the war, President John F. Kennedy, realizing the need for a special operations team to be available for any situation that may arise, signed into existence what became the Sea, Air and Land Teams, or what you know as the Navy SEALs. In the process, the UDT divers and Draper Kauffman's training, culture, and lessons became the backbone of SEAL training. In the years that followed, these frogmen became the gold standard for military operators, taking on many of the most famous public missions, from the rescuing of Captain Richard Phillips to the takedown of Osama bin Laden.

Much like a team's success, war is won not by one lone hero, but by countless contributions small and large toward a mission. When we do our jobs, the truth is we will never know about most of the contributions people make. In conversations with Draper's family, they shared how little he cared for recognition and attention. What truly mattered to him was his men. He would have likely been really uncomfortable with me dedicating an entire chapter of this book to his career, but I had never come across someone who embodied the ideas of leadership and teams so perfectly. Through his efforts he was able to create one of the most effective organizational cultures that still stands today. Thanks to his contributions, the UDT divers and later the Navy SEALs played an incredible role in our history.

This all happened because some unstoppable glue player, a US Naval Academy graduate, didn't get a position in the Navy because of his bad eyesight and instead learned a series of lessons. As volunteer ambulance driver, the Corps Franc showed him that a leader's job is to ensure the connections between their team members, and from the nun, he saw the benefits of leaning into his super skills. When volunteering as a bomb defuser, he learned that courage is found in the service of a greater goal and that teams that are aligned around that goal are more effective. From Captain Currey he learned the importance of synchronized bursty communication and instilling competence in his men, so they could make great decisions, especially at a distance. With his men he saw that the diversity of resources created better solutions faster.

These lessons were at the heart of his training and the way he led, from the trust created by having officers and enlisted men train together to embodying the characteristics of team intelligence (reasoning, attention, and resources) to having the teams operate independently so they could make their own calls as they were working remotely. Draper embodied everything that researchers would later discover creates effective leaders and teams, and as a result, his men delivered. As you've probably learned from spending eleven chapters in my brain, I love a good twist, so the best part of the story for me was when I discovered that the very same Draper L. Kauffman who graduated from the Naval Academy but couldn't get a commission in the Navy would go on to become the forty-fourth superintendent of the Academy. It's like reconnecting with your high school crush at the reunion, only now you're successful, and suddenly they're into you. I felt an odd sense of satisfaction knowing that a person who cared so much for his team would be shaping the lives of future leaders and sailors.

Now we have an opportunity to take the ideas in this book, so beautifully embodied by Draper, and apply them to impact our teams and the way we lead. Am I saying you should make SEAL training your next company bonding activity? No, and if you genuinely thought that was where I was going with this, then I shudder to think what other terrible lessons you've accidentally learned from my book. If we want to succeed at anything that is important to us, from business to impacting social causes or our health and happiness, we need to understand that what allows leaders and teams to operate at their best are actually the things that are most human. And fortunately, "being human" isn't one of those roles that requires a year of experience just to get an entry-level job. The fact that you're you is qualifying enough. So, I leave you with this.

From what I have learned about Draper I think he would agree that although this story sounds larger-than-life, he was an ordinary person. He had no superhuman skills. Instead he was a scrawny, practically blind ambulance driver working in rural France in World War II. It should fill you with confidence that if he could redefine culture, there is little doubt in my mind that you can be an incredible leader and team member. You can be the person that leans into your super skills, connects people, and brings out their collective genius. You can be the glue that unlocks your team intelligence, making it far greater than the sum of its parts. You got this!

Acknowledgments

Wow! This part of the book always sneaks up on me. I have done this two times before, and I never know the right words to express how much I appreciate everyone's support. I also want to keep this short enough that people will actually read it. This means I don't have time to talk about the most beloved agent in the publishing industry, James Levine—everyone who works with him, me especially, can't stop talking about what a supportive, smart, and wonderful person he is. I absolutely can't take time sharing what a delight it is to work with Hollis Heimbouch, my publisher, whose companionate ruthlessness made this book half as long and twice as good, and she picked a great title. There is no time to acknowledge all the incredible people at Harper Business who edited, packaged, produced, sold, and distributed my book, or Andrew Moorhead from Hello SciCom, who helped me make the book a bit more lighthearted. But if I did have a few more minutes of your time, I would mention the brilliant creative mind of Rodrigo Corral, my cover designer, who had to put up with my insane ideas and was able to create the beauty you are holding right now.

Since we don't have the time, I will skip thanking my wife, Dasha, who had to put up with me repeating my stories countless times until I found the ones that work, and my lovely children, who reminded me that even if this book stinks that's okay, because all they want is to play, laugh, and dance with me.

I might be able to skip my wife and kids, but I absolutely need to make time to thank the people who got me unstuck along the way. There is a special place writers know where we have gone down a path so far we don't know if we are lost in an idea or about to hit gold, so we call on our trusted advisers, in my case David Burkus, and, yes, you too, Shane Snow. Fortunately, I can save time by skipping Nick Sonnenberg, Blake Eastman, and Liam Alexander, since they barely helped getting me unstuck (LOL).

We can also save a ton of time by not saying thank you to all the incredible C-suite executives and friends who made time to be interviewed or just have a conversation. Getting to hear your opinions, insights, experience, and stories was absolutely critical to shaping this book. I wanted to express my appreciation by putting your name here, and then I realized that our conversation was off the record. Hopefully if you see this, you know I am talking to you. Thank you! The few of you who were on the record, like William Muir, Ramani Durvasula, Joe Price, Shane Battier, Trafton Drew, Jeffrey Pfeffer, L. David Mech, Duff McDonald, Erica R. Bailey, Sandra Matz, Terry Virts, Justin "Hasard" Lee, Seth Stephens-Davidowitz, Neil Paine, Todd Kahn, and William Nadeau, I don't need to acknowledge, even though I loved our conversations.

Lastly, I know my life is as great as it is because of two groups, first the people who come and cook me dinner. The Influencers community members who have befriended me around terrible food. Thank you for everything; it is a true privilege to know you. And, most importantly, the people who raised me: my mother, Hanna Levy, and my late father, Benjamin Levy, and all of my siblings, Ofer, Bat-Sheva, and Amnon. I was given more support and love than any child could need. If I had a choice of what family to be born to, even with all our ridiculous quirks, I don't think I could have had it any better.

One person I always knew I would make time for in the acknowledgments is Luke Skywalker, for putting Darth Vader in his place. Some bosses just need to be set straight.

THANK YOU ALL!

Notes

Brilliant Leaders Start Here

5   *true for smoking, voting:* Nicholas Christakis, *The Hidden Influence of Social Networks*, filmed May 2010, TED Video, 8:17, https://www.youtube.com/watch?v=2U-tOghblfE.

9   *don't notice the giant gorilla:* Trafton Drew, Melissa L-H Võ, and Jeremy M. Wolfe, "The Invisible Gorilla Strikes Again: Sustained Inattentional Blindness in Expert Observers," *Psychological Science* 24, no. 9 (2013): 1848–53.

9   *inattentional blindness:* Arien Mack and Irvin Rock, *Inattentional Blindness* (Cambridge, MA: MIT Press, 1998).

13 *impact on leadership performance:* Barbara Kellerman, *Professionalizing Leadership* (New York: Oxford University Press, 2018).

Chapter 1: Mis-Leading

22 *"the ones calling the shots":* Kate Ludeman and Eddie Erlandson, "Coaching the Alpha Male," *Harvard Business Review*, May 2004, https://hbr.org/2004/05/coaching-the-alpha-male.

22 *control through domination and intimidation:* L. David Mech, *The Wolf: The Ecology and Behavior of an Endangered Species* (Minneapolis: University of Minnesota Press, 1981).

24 *a few fun quotes:* Michael O'Leary "Quotefancy," 2024, https://quotefancy.com/michael-o-leary-quotes.

25 *200 million customers a year:* "Ryanair: Cheap, Cramped and Making Its CEO a Fortune," *The Journal*, WSJ Podcasts, April 2024, https://www.wsj.com/podcasts/the-journal/ryanair-cheap-cramped-and-making-its-ceo-a-fortune/f4678238-4f61-4cdf-b3a3-5980def7ecbf.

25 *"glad I don't work for them":* Ludeman and Erlandson, "Coaching the Alpha Male."

26 *make for better negotiators:* Adam Grant, "In Negotiations, Givers Are Smarter Than Takers," *New York Times*, March 27, 2020, https://www.nytimes.com/2020/03/27/smarter-living/negotiation-tips-giver-taker.html.

27 *what makes a great leader:* Kellerman, *Professionalizing Leadership*.

28 *"turn ourselves into machines":* Phone interview conducted by author with Duff McDonald, April 15, 2024.

29 *"father of scientific management":* Sean Peek, "The Management Theory of Elton Mayo,"

business.com, January 14, 2025, https://www.business.com/articles/management-theory-of-elton-mayo/

29 *just been watching people:* Duff McDonald, *The Golden Passport: Harvard Business School, the Limits of Capitalism, and the Moral Failure of the MBA Elite* (New York: HarperCollins, 2017).

30 *"correlate with career success":* Jeffrey Pfeffer and Christina T. Fong, "The End of Business Schools? Less Success than Meets the Eye," *Academy of Management Learning & Education* 1, no. 1 (2002): 78–9.

30 *"successful as those with the degree":* Pfeffer and Fong, "The End of Business Schools?"

30 *"who had gone to business school":* David Leonhardt, "A Matter of Degree? Not for Consultants," *New York Times*, October 1, 2000, https://www.nytimes.com/2000/10/01/business/a-matter-of-degree-not-for-consultants.html.

30 *"top-notch liberal arts programs":* Ron Lieber, "Learning and Change—Roger Martin," *Fast Company*, Nov 30, 1999, https://www.fastcompany.com/39166/learning-and-change-roger-martin.

31 *eight different personality types:* "Psychological Types," Wikipedia, last modified October 23, 2024, https://en.wikipedia.org/wiki/Psychological_Types.

32 *"Every individual is an exception to the rule":* Quote Investigator, "Every Individual Is an Exception to the Rule," 2018, https://quoteinvestigator.com/2018/04/18/exception/.

32 *no clear understanding of science:* Myers & Briggs Foundation, "Evolving the MBTI Legacy," https://myersbriggs.org.

32 *Who am I?:* Merve Emre, *The Personality Brokers: The Strange History of Myers-Briggs and the Birth of Personality Testing* (New York: Doubleday, 2018).

32 *Perceiving (P) by adapting more:* Myers-Briggs Company, Myers-Briggs Type Indicator assessment, https://www.themyersbriggs.com/en-US/.

33 *to train, develop, hire, fire, and place employees:* Emre, *The Personality Brokers*.

34 *average accuracy rating was 4.3:* D. L. Dutton, "The Cold Reading Technique," *Experientia* 44, no. 4 (1988): 326–32.

34 *done the right thing:* Bertram R. Forer, "The Fallacy of Personal Validation: A Classroom Demonstration of Gullibility," *Journal of Abnormal and Social Psychology* 44, no. 1 (1949): 118–23, https://doi.org/10.1037/h0059240.

35 *"specific applications to oneself":* "Barnum effect," APA Dictionary of Psychology, American Psychological Association, April 19, 2018, https://dictionary.apa.org barnum-effect.

35 *were in full control:* "Frequency Illusion," Wikipedia, December 21, 2024, https://en.wikipedia.org/wiki/Frequency_illusion.

35 *study after study:* William L. Gardner and Mark J. Martinko, "Using the Myers-Briggs Type Indicator to Study Managers: A Literature Review and Research Agenda," *Journal of Management* 22, no. 1 (1996): 45–83.

35 *useless at predicting anything:* David Pittenger: "Cautionary Comments Regarding the

Myers-Briggs Type Indicator," *Consulting Psychology Journal Practice and Research* 57, no. 3 (2005): 210–221.

35 *five weeks later:* David J. Pittenger, "Measuring the MBTI and Coming Up Short," https://jobtalk.indiana.edu/HRMWebsite/hrm/articles/develop/mbti.pdf.

35 *from one hour to the next:* Francine Russo, "Personality Can Change from One Hour to the Next," *Scientific American*, April 5, 2023, https://www.scientificamerican.com/article/personality-can-change-from-one-hour-to-the-next/.

39 *different behaviors emerge:* Amanda Aronczyk and Bethel Habte, "Driverless Dilemma," *Radiolab* (podcast), September 26, 2017, https://radiolab.org/podcast/driverless-dilemma.

39 *didn't match each other:* Erica R. Bailey and Aharon Levy, "Are You for Real? Perceptions of Authenticity Are Systematically Biased and Not Accurate," *Psychological Science* 33, no. 5 (2022): 798–815.

40 *more "authentic":* William Hart et al., "To Be or to Appear to Be: Evidence That Authentic People Seek to Appear Authentic Rather Than Be Authentic," *Personality and Individual Differences* 166 (2020).

Chapter 2: Why Should Anyone Follow You?

44 *the local chief's feasts:* Lee Alan Dugatkin, *The Imitation Factor: Evolution Beyond the Gene* (New York: Free Press, 2000).

44 *sheer size of a man's yam:* William R. Bascom, "Ponapean Prestige Economy," *Southwestern Journal of Anthropology* 4, no. 2 (1948): 211–21.

44 *According to Bascom:* Bascom.

44 *publicly shamed:* Bascom.

44 *"shame of gossip and ridicule":* Bascom.

45 *$15 million:* Lisa Fleisher and Low De Wei, "World's Most Expensive Car License Plate Sells for Record $15 Million in Dubai," Bloomberg, April 10, 2023, https://www.bloomberg.com/news/articles/2023-04-10/world-s-most-expensive-car-license-plate-sells-for-15-million-in-dubai.

46 *three million people in the region died:* Senjuti Mallik, "Colonial Biopolitics and the Great Bengal Famine of 1943," *Geographical Journal* 88, no. 3 (2023): 3205–21.

47 *"abandoned by their families":* "Commemorative Coin on Mother Teresa Released," *Times of India*, August 28, 2010.

47 *760 homes in 139 countries:* "Mother Teresa Nuns Face Probe over Funding Allegations," UCA News, September 5, 2018, https://www.ucanews.com/news/mother-teresa-nuns-face-probe-over-funding-allegations/85463.

49 *newspaper articles:* Christopher Hitchens, *The Missionary Position: Mother Teresa in Theory and Practice* (London: Atlantic Books, 2012); Kamdev, *Mother Teresa: The Dark Truth*, July 3, 2023, YouTube, https://www.youtube.com/watch?v=Nactsb2bZeo.

49 *caring for the poor and sick:* Mallika Kapur and Sugam Pokharel, " 'Troubled Individual': Mother Teresa No Saint to Her Critics," CNN, September 4, 2016, https://edition.cnn.com/2016/08/31/asia/mother-teresa-controversies/index.html.

49 *washed in water (not sterilized):* Geneviève Chénard, "Should Mother Teresa Be Canonized?" *New York Times*, March 25, 2016, https://www.nytimes.com/roomfordebate/2016/03/25/should-mother-teresa-be-canonized/mother-teresa-doesnt-deserve-sainthood.

49 *would perform the ritual:* Hitchens, *The Missionary Position*.

49 *"He can kiss you":* Goodreads, https://www.goodreads.com/quotes/216250-pain-and-suffering-have-come-into-your-life-but-remember.

51 *"numbers became my best friends":* Paul Hoffman, *The Man Who Loved Only Numbers: The Story of Paul Erdös and the Search for Mathematical Truth* (New York: Grand Central, 1998).

52 *"My brain is open":* "From Benford to Erdös," *Radiolab* (podcast), August 19, 2020, https://radiolab.org/podcast/91699-from-benford-to-erdos.

52 *to do more work:* Hoffman, *The Man Who Loved Only Numbers*.

54 *"transcends the physical universe":* Gina Kolata, "Paul Erdos, 83, a Wayfarer in Math's Vanguard, Is Dead," *New York Times*, September 24, 1996, https://www.nytimes.com/1996/09/24/us/paul-erdos-83-a-wayfarer-in-math-s-vanguard-is-dead.html.

55 *her resoluteness and incorruptibility:* "The Wangari Muta Maathai House—A Legacy Project," Green Belt Movement, https://www.greenbeltmovement.org/node/714.

55 *"believed in the mission":* Tim Higgins and Kate Linebaugh, "Elon Musk's 'Demon Mode,'" *The Journal* (podcast), *Wall Street Journal*, September 12, 2023, https://www.wsj.com/podcasts/the-journal/elon-musk-demon-mode/69f38af7-7caf-47e2-b853-14448d807909.

Chapter 3: Growing Your Skills

62 *"groin kick":* Bailey Bassett, "15 Dirtiest Players in NBA History, Ranked," ClutchPoints, December 17, 2024.

62 *to underperform the following year:* Kate McGreavy, "Draymond Green says he 'DOESN'T CARE' about backlash to his brutal sucker-punch on Warriors teammate Jordan Poole - and that he had no idea people were mad about it because he doesn't check social media," *Daily Mail*, October 19, 2022, https://www.dailymail.co.uk/sport/nba/article-11330167/Draymond-Green-reflects-punching-Warriors-teammate-Jordan-Poole.html.

63 *it was psychological safety:* Charles Duhigg, "What Google Learned from Its Quest to Build the Perfect Team," *New York Times Magazine*, February 25, 2016, https://www.nytimes.com/2016/02/28/magazine/what-google-learned-from-its-quest-to-build-the-perfect-team.html.

63 *fear of being punished or pushed:* Duhigg.

64 *more likely to be the victims:* International Labour Organization, "Violence and Harassment Against Women and Men in the World of Work," 2017, https://www.ilo.org/sites/default/files/wcmsp5/groups/public/@ed_dialogue/@actrav/documents/publication/wcms_546645.pdf.

64 *harassment at work:* Steve Crabtree, "Global Study: 23% of Workers Experience Violence, Harassment," Gallup, December 14, 2022, https://news.gallup.com/opinion/gallup/406793/global-study-workers-experience-violence-harassment.aspx; "Measuring #MeToo: A National Study on Sexual Harassment and Assault," Raliance, 2019, https://www.raliance.org/wp-content/uploads/2019/04/2019-MeToo-National-Sexual-Harassment-and-Assault-Report.pdf.

66 *F-16 pilot deaths:* "Falcon Forward: A New Era of F-16," Lockheed Martin, https://www.lockheedmartin.com/en-us/products/f-16.html.

69 *hours they practiced alone:* Karl Ericsson et al., "The Role of Deliberate Practice in Acquisition of Expert Performance," *Psychological Review* 100, no. 3 (1993): 363–406.

70 *"not as important as has been argued":* Brooke N. Macnamara et al., "Deliberate Practice and Performance in Music, Games, Sports, Education and Professions: A Meta-Analysis," *Psychological Science* 25, no. 8 (2014): 1608–18.

71 *20,000 hours of practice:* Guillermo Campitelli and Fernand Gobet, "Deliberate Practice: Necessary but Not Sufficient," *Current Directions in Psychological Science* 20, no. 5 (2011): 28–85.

73 *Vladimir Makogonov:* Stephen Ham, "The Young King," Chess Cafe, retrieved November 30, 2006.

73 *Alexander Nikitin:* Alexander Nikitin, *Coaching Kasparov: Year by Year and Move by Move,* vol. 1, *The Whizz-Kid (1973–1981)* (UK: Elk and Ruby, 2019).

73 *Alexander Shakarov:* "Harry—The Child Prodigy and the Genius of the Game," *Science & Life*, 1976, https://www.nkj.ru/archive/articles/2158/.

74 *versus those who just did training:* Gerald Olivero et al., "Executive Coaching as a Transfer of Training Tool: Effects on Productivity in Public Agency," *Public Personnel Management* 26, no. 4 (1997).

74 *achieved more when being coached:* Qing Wang et al., "The Effectiveness of Workplace Coaching: A Meta-Analysis of Contemporary Psychologically Informed Coaching Approaches," *Journal of Work-Applied Management* 14, no. 1 (2022): 77–101.

74 *5 percent increase:* Nicholas A. Christakis and James H. Fowler, "The Spread of Obesity in a Large Social Network over 32 Years," *New England Journal of Medicine* 357, no. 4 (2007): 370–79.

74 *contagious through a social group:* Nicholas Christakis, "The Hidden Influence of Social Networks," TED Talk, February 2010, https://www.ted.com/talks/nicholas_christakis_the_hidden_influence_of_social_networks.

76 *disconnected from reality:* NCAA Research, "Five Themes from the NCAA GOALS

Study of the Student-Athlete Experience," 2019, https://ncaaorg.s3.amazonaws.com/research/goals/2020D1RES_GOALS2020con.pdf.

Chapter 4: Welcome to the Team

85 *they were stronger than us:* Lisa Hendry, "Who Were the Neanderthals," Natural History Museum, London, https://www.nhm.ac.uk/discover/who-were-the-neanderthals.html.

85 *at least as smart:* University of Trento, "20-Year Study Reveals: Neanderthals Were as Intelligent as *Homo Sapiens*," SciTechDaily, October 15, 2023, https://scitechdaily.com/20-year-study-reveals-neanderthals-were-as-intelligent-as-homo-sapiens/.

86 *will scale too fast:* "106 Must-Known Startup Statistics for 2024," Embroker, January 23, 2025, https://www.embroker.com/blog/startup-statistics/.

87 *results were comedic:* Alan Benson et al., "Promotions and the Peter Principle," National Bureau of Economic Research, 2018.

89 *record for running across the US:* Kit Fox, "Ultrarunner Pete Kostelnick Smashes Record for Run Across U.S.," *Runners World*, October 24, 2016, https://www.runnersworld.com/news/a20828478/ultrarunner-pete-kostelnick-smashes-record-for-run-across-u-s/.

90 *could maneuver on them at speed: The Creation of America's Highway System*, History, "The Engineering That Built the World" (Season 1), October 27, 2021, https://www.youtube.com/watch?v=OHZukqaRdoA.

91 *cross-country military convoy:* Christopher Klein, "The Epic Road Trip That Inspired the Interstate Highway System," History, June 28, 2024, https://www.history.com/news/the-epic-road-trip-that-inspired-the-interstate-highway-system.

93 *"when they have that coach":* Interview with Seth Stephens-Davidowitz, February 13, 2024.

94 *"early season performance":* Michael W. Kraus et al., "Tactile Communication, Cooperation and Performance: An Ethological Study of the NBA," *Emotion* 10, no. 5 (2010): 745–49.

94 *"head slaps, head grabs":* Stephanie Pappas, "Touchy-Feely NBA Teams More Likely to Win," Live Science, November 9, 2010, https://www.livescience.com/11091-touchy-feely-nba-teams-win.html.

96 *less likely to keep their jobs:* Mitch Prinstein, "Does Our High School Popularity Affect Us Today?" TEDx Talks, March 22, 2019, https://www.youtube.com/watch?v=L7e_xs4KBVY&t=2s.

98 *because they have to assemble it:* Michael I. Norton, "The 'IKEA Effect': When Labor Leads to Love," 2011.

99 *vulnerability loop:* Interview with Dr. Jeff Polzer.

100 *outranked those who were perfect:* Elliot Aronson et al., "The Effect of Pratfall on Increasing Interpersonal Attractiveness," *Psychonomic Science* 4 (1966): 227–28.

Chapter 5: Super Chickens (The Too-Much-Talent Problem)

103 *too-much-talent problem:* Roderick I. Swaab et al., "The Too-Much-Talent Effect: Team Interdependence Determines When More Talent Is Too Much or Not Enough," *Psychological Science* 25, no. 8 (2014): 1581–91.

103 *talent across different sports:* Swaab et al.

104 *"task interdependence":* Swaab et al.

106 *he could repeat the process:* W. M. Muir, "Group Selection for Adaptation to Multiple-Hen Cages: Selection Program and Direct Responses," *Poultry Science* 785, no 4 (1996): 447–58.

106 *productivity and prosocial behavior:* W. M. Muir, "Relative Efficiency of Selection for Performance of Birds Housed in Colony Cages Based on Production in Single Bird Cages," *Poultry Science* 64 (1985): 2239–47.

106 *Muir ran two competitions:* Muir, "Relative Efficiency."

107 *pecked to death:* J. V. Craig and W. M. Muir, "Group Selection for Adaptation to Multiple-Hen Cages: Beak-Related Mortality, Feathering, and Body Weight Responses," *Poultry Science* 7, no. 3 (1996): 294–302.

107 *continuing to produce:* W. M. Muir and Heng Wei Cheng, "Genetic Influences on the Behavior of Chickens Associated with Welfare and Productivity," *Academic Press* (2019): 317–59.

107 *productivity and sociability:* Muir, "Group Selection for Adaptation to Multiple-Hen Cages: Selection Program and Direct Responses."

109 *points scored:* Seth Stephens-Davidowitz, *Who Makes the NBA? Data-Driven Answers to Basketball's Biggest Questions* (ebook, 2023).

110 *no sense of security or stability:* Alana Semuels, "How the Relationship Between Employers and Workers Changed," *Los Angeles Times*, April 7, 2013, https://www.latimes.com/business/la-fi-mo-harsh-work-history-20130405-story.html.

113 *"hasn't got much body control":* Michael Lewis, "The No-Stats All-Star," *New York Times Magazine*, February 13, 2009, https://www.nytimes.com/2009/02/15/magazine/15Battier-t.html.

115 *A-Team or Three's Company:* Shane Battier, "Elite 'Glue Guys' 101," *Player's Tribune*, February 18, 2016, https://www.theplayerstribune.com/articles/elite-glue-guys-101.

115 *"they'll like you":* Battier, "Elite 'Glue Guys' 101."

115 *"credit the team got":* Battier.

117 *"violate his own personal interests":* Lewis.

118 *"when I say that I really believe it":* m3lomanUP, "LeBron James Says the Heat Will Win 7 Titles," YouTube, July 11, 2010, https://www.youtube.com/watch?v=EYe8B--jrbs.

118 *sell out stadiums:* Kurt Helin, "Heat Players Nickname Themselves 'the Heatles,'"

NBC Sports, January 4, 2011, https://www.nbcsports.com/nba/news/heat-players-nickname-themselves-the-heatles.

119 *much like Shane Battier:* Neil Paine et al., "2014 NBA Preview: The Rise of the Warriors," FiveThirtyEight, October 24, 2014, https://fivethirtyeight.com/features/2014-nba-preview-the-rise-of-the-warriors/.

119 *"how team basketball should be played":* Jeff Zillgitt, "LeBron James on Blame: 'Obviously I Didn't Do Enough,'" *USA Today*, June 26, 2014, https://www.usatoday.com/story/sports/nba/playoffs/2014/06/16/lebron-james-future-miami-heat-vs-san-antonio-spurs-game-5-finals/10568473/.

119 *Cavaliers for more pay:* Shandel Richardson, "LeBron James Reportedly Declined Pat Riley's Request to Play for Less Money in 2024," *Sports Illustrated*, July 23, 2022, https://www.si.com/nba/heat/miami-news/lebron-james-reportedly-declined-pat-rileys-request-to-play-for-less-money-in-2014.

Chapter 6: Team Intelligence—Reasoning

123 *crushing the escape room:* Anita Williams Woolley et al., "Evidence for a Collective Intelligence Factor in the Performance of Human Groups," *Science* 330, no. 6004 (2010): 686–88.

124 *item availability:* Anita Williams Woolley, "Collective Intelligence in Human Groups," 2013, https://sonic.northwestern.edu/wp-content/uploads/2013/09/04.-Anita-Collective-Intelligence-NSF-Network-Science-October-2013.pdf.

126 *jam signals using satellites:* Brett Tingley, "Space Force Tests Small Satellite Jammer to Protect Against 'Space Enabled' Attacks," Space.com, April 24, 2024, https://www.space.com/space-force-ground-based-jammer-electronic-warfare.

127 *60 percent of them found it unmotivating:* Val Matta, "Do Your Employees Know Your Mission Statemet? This Is Why It's Important," Career Shift, August 29, 2016, https://careershift.com/blog/2016/08/do-employees-know-your-mission-statement/.

127 *$450 billion and $550 billion a year:* "Gallup Releases New Findings on the State of the American Workplace," Gallup, June 11, 2013, https://news.gallup.com/opinion/gallup/170570/gallup-releases-new-findings-state-american-workplace.aspx.

Chapter 7: Team Intelligence—Attention

135 *parent has just stepped on one:* Christine Chen and Tim Carvell, "Products of the Century in 1900," CNN Money, November 22, 1999.

136 *"strongest brand":* "Innovation Almost Bankrupted LEGO—Until It Rebuilt with a Better Blueprint," Knowledge at Wharton, July 18, 2022, https://knowledge.wharton.upenn.edu/article/innovation-almost-bankrupted-lego-until-it-rebuilt-with-a-better-blueprint/?utm_source=chatgpt.com.

137 *"focus, as much as creativity":* David Robertson with Bill Breen, *Brick by Brick: How LEGO*

Rewrote the Rules of Innovation and Conquered the Global Toy Industry (New York: Crown Currency, 2014).

140 *brain waves begin to align:* Uri Hasson et al., "Brain-to-Brain Coupling: A Mechanism for Creating and Sharing a Social Word," *Trends in Cognitive Science* 16, no. 2 (2012): 114–21.

140 *neural entrainment:* Uri Hasson, "This Is Your Brain on Communication," TED Talks, February 2016, https://www.ted.com/talks/uri_hasson_this_is_your_brain_on_communication.

142 *tests your empathy:* Amie M. Gordon, "Are You a Good 'Mind-Reader'?" *Psychology Today*, May 30, 2014, https://www.psychologytoday.com/au/blog/between-you-and-me/201405/are-you-a-good-mind-reader.

144 *"respect and trust among team members":* Amy Edmondson, "Psychological Safety and Learning Behavior in Work Teams," *Administrative Science Quarterly* 44, no. 2 (1999): 350–83.

145 *more potential safety issues:* Lindsay Thompson Munn et al., "A Study of Error Reporting by Nurses: The Significant Impact of Nursing Team Dynamics," *Journal of Research in Nursing* 28, no. 5 (2023): 354–64.

Chapter 9: The Good and the Bad

170 *characteristics of a psychopath:* Robert D. Hare, *Without Conscience: The Disturbing World of the Psychopaths Among Us* (New York: Guilford Press, 1999).

170 *"some were in the boardroom":* Robert D. Hare, quoted in Jon Ronson, *The Psychopath Test: A Journey Through the Madness Industry* (New York: Riverhead Books, 2011).

170 *Great British Psychopath Survey:* Kevin Dutton, *The Wisdom of Psychopaths: What Saints, Spies, and Serial Killers Can Teach Us About Success* (New York: Scientific American / Farrar, Straus and Giroux, 2012).

171 *0.5–5 percent of the population:* Jean M. Twenge and W. Keith Campbell, *The Narcissism Epidemic: Living in the Age of Entitlement* (New York: Free Press, 2009).

171 *as high as 10 percent of the population:* Twenge and Campbell, *The Narcissism Epidemic*.

171 *30 percent increase in narcissism scores:* Jean M. Twenge, "Generational Changes and Their Impact in the Classroom: Teaching Generation Me," *Medical Education* 43, no. 5 (2009): 398–405.

171 *77–80 percent in 1992:* Jean M. Twenge, *Generation Me: Why Today's Young Americans Are More Confident, Assertive, Entitled—and More Miserable Than Ever Before* (New York: Atria Books, 2014).

171 *you and your quadrupled:* Twenge, *Generation Me*.

172 *"use that knowledge to manipulate them":* Joseph Burgo, *The Narcissist You Know: Defending Yourself Against Extreme Narcissists in an All-About-Me Age* (New York: Touchstone, 2016).

172 *DARVO:* Jennifer J. Freyd, "Violations of Power, Adaptive Blindness and Betrayal Trauma Theory," *Feminism & Psychology* 7, no. 1 (1997): 22–32.

174 *"over repeated exposure":* Delroy L. Paulhus, "Interpersonal and Intrapsychic Adaptiveness of Trait Self-Enhancement: A Mixed Blessing?" *Journal of Personality and Social Psychology* 74, no. 5 (1998): 1197–1208.

174 *"drawn to success and money":* Ramani S. Durvasula, *"Don't You Know Who I Am?": How to Stay Sane in an Era of Narcissism, Entitlement, and Incivility* (New York: Post Hill Press, 2019).

178 *work faster and be more productive:* Alexandre Mas and Enrico Moretti, "Peers at Work," *American Economic Review* 99, no. 1 (2009): 112–45.

178 *easier pitches and perform better:* Eric D. Gould and Eyal Winter, "Interactions Between Workers and the Technology of Production: Evidence from Professional Baseball," *Review of Economics and Statistics* 91, no. 1 (2009): 188–200.

179 *easy-to-measure statistics:* Gould and Winter.

Chapter 10: Welcome to the Corporate Family

187 *changed the direction of business:* Milton Friedman, "A Friedman Doctrine: The Social Responsibility of Business Is to Increase Its Profits," *New York Times*, September 13, 1970, https://www.nytimes.com/1970/09/13/archives/a-friedman-doctrine-the-social-responsibility-of-business-is-to.html.

188 *"designed to increase its profits":* Friedman.

188 *faking emission standards:* Russell Hotten, "Volkswagen: The Scandal Explained," BBC News, December 10, 2015, https://www.bbc.com/news/business-34324772.

189 *"phenomenally talented":* Maureen Tkacik, "Suicide Mission: What Boeing Did to All the Guys Who Remember How to Build a Plane," *American Prospect*, March 28, 2024, https://prospect.org/infrastructure/transportation/2024-03-28-suicide-mission-boeing/.

190 *Dreamliner, knowing how it was built:* Will Jordan, "Exclusive: Safety Concerns Dog Boeing 787," Al Jazeera, September 8, 2014, https://www.aljazeera.com/economy/2014/9/8/exclusive-safety-concerns-dog-boeing-787.

190 *consumed $70 billion:* Stan Sorscher, "What Will It Be, Boeing?" *Seattle Times*, July 5, 2019, https://www.seattletimes.com/opinion/what-will-it-be-boeing-great-airplanes-that-generate-cash-flow-or-great-cash-flow-period/.

191 *buyback at $20 billion:* Jullie Johnson, "Boeing Sets New $20 Billion Buyback Plan, Raises 20% Dividend," Bloomberg, December 18, 2018, https://www.bloomberg.com/news/articles/2018-12-17/boeing-sets-new-20-billion-buyback-plan-raises-dividend-20.

191 *safety process:* Lauren Rosenblatt, "After Months Hearing About Safety from Boeing Workers, a Call for Change," *Seattle Times*, April 17, 2024, https://www.seattletimes

192 .com/business/boeing-workers-still-scared-to-raise-safety-concerns-says-faa-appointed-experts/.

192 *half of what it was at its peak:* "The Boeing Company," Stock Analysis, January 24, 2025, https://stockanalysis.com/stocks/ba/market-cap/.

192 *"heart of corporate leadership":* "The Error at the Heart of Corporate Leadership," *Harvard Business Review*, 2017, https://hbr.org/2017/05/the-error-at-the-heart-of-corporate-leadership.

192 *wasn't focusing on stock value:* John Asker et al., "Corporate Investment and Stock Market Listing: A Puzzle?" *Review of Financial Studies* 28, no. 2 (2015): 342–90.

193 *"long-term value":* Francesco Guerrera, "Welch Condemns Share Price Focus," *Financial Times*, March 12, 2009, https://www.ft.com/content/294ff1f2-0f27-11de-ba10-0000779fd2ac#axzz1eiLpL2PZ.

193 *installs it on the plane:* Gregory Wallace, "Former Boeing Inspector Alleges 'Scrap' Parts Ended Up on Assembly Lines," CNN, July 3, 2024, https://edition.cnn.com/2024/07/03/business/former-boeing-inspector-scrap-parts-assembly-lines/index.html.

195 *after their training period:* Stephanie Vozza, "This CEO Pays New Employees $5,000 to Quit," *Fast Company*, May 1, 2022, https://www.fastcompany.com/90708440/this-ceo-pays-new-employees-5000-to-quit.

197 *"calls us entitled":* "Google Employees Are Called Googlers, Amazon Employees Are Called Amazonians," Team Blind, April 28, 2022, https://www.teamblind.com/post/Google-employees-are-called-Googlers-Amazon-employees-are-called-Amazonians-16CGE5dF.

199 *"low-cost air travel":* "About Southwest Airlines," Southwest Airlines, https://www.southwest.com/about-southwest/.

200 *strict denominations:* Judith Shulevitz, "The Power of Mustard Seed," *Slate*, May 12, 2005, https://slate.com/human-interest/2005/05/why-strict-churches-are-strong.html.

201 *"high cultural fit":* Matthew Corritore, Amir Goldberg, and Sameer B. Srivastava, "The New Analytics of Culture," *Harvard Business Review*, January 2020.

202 *company probably didn't sell:* "The Nordy Pod: The Truth About Nordstrom's Legendary Tire Story," Nordstrom, https://press.nordstrom.com/news-releases/news-release-details/nordy-pod-truth-about-nordstroms-legendary-tire-story.

205 *$15 million profit:* Alex "Sandy" Pentland, "The New Science of Building Great Teams," *Harvard Business Review*, April 2012.

Chapter 11: Becoming the Leader We Need

215 *"paid no attention to bureaucracy":* Elizabeth Kauffman Bush, *America's First Frogman: The Draper Kauffman Story* (Annapolis, MD: Naval Institute Press, 2004).

215 *"over anyone else":* Kauffman Bush.

217 *"we all admired Draper Kauffman":* Kauffman Bush.

Index

accountability, 73–74
advantages, natural, 71–73, 82
aggressiveness, 21–26, 42
Airbnb, 2
Airbus, 190
Alaska Airlines, 191
Allen, Paul, 70
alpha mentality, 21–26, 42
Amazon, 196
antagonistic narcissists, 172
Anthony, Carmelo, 2
Antwerp Diamond Center, 153–158, 161–162
Apple, 40, 174–175
artificial intelligence (AI), 204
attention
   emotional intelligence and, 141–144, 149
   psychological safety and, 144–146, 149–150, 195
   rewarding habits that create, 150–151
   shifting, 139–140, 147–148
   in team intelligence, 125, 138–139, 162, 208, 219
attitude, 75–77
authenticity, 36–41, 42
autism, 141–142
Auto G-Cas (Ground Collision Avoidance System), 67
automatic systems, 67–68

Bailey, Erica R., 39
Barnum effect. *See* Forer effect
Baron-Cohen, Simon, 141–142
Bascom, William R., 44
baseball, 104–105
basketball
   getting teams to stick together, 113–120
   glue players, 114–115, 119–120, 122, 123, 143, 167, 178–182
   Green's behavior management, 61–62, 68–69
   multiplier effect, 179–180
   NBA All-Stars, 1–2, 10, 61, 109
   plus-minus stats, 114–115
   success metrics, 93–94, 109
   Team USA, 1–2, 10, 109, 118
   too-much-talent problem, 103
Battier, Shane, 113–119, 121–122, 143, 161, 167, 180
behaviors
   authenticity and, 38–39
   changing, 66–67
   contagious, 5, 74–75, 79, 80
   DARVO, 172
   documentation of, 177–178
   effects of negative, 62–65
   Forer effect, 34–35
   Hawthorne effect, 29
   prosocial, 167
   synchronized, 140, 148
   wolves, 22–23
belonging, sense of, 93–94, 96, 196–197
benevolence, 96, 181, 217–218
Bill & Melinda Gates Foundation, 54
bin Laden, Osama, 220
Black Lives Matter movement, 40
Boeing, 188–192, 193, 200
Bogues, Muggsy, 71–72
Bojaxhiu, Anjezë Gonxhe, 46. *See also* Mother Teresa

Index

Bombas, 198
Bosh, Chris, 118
Boston Consulting Group (BCG), 30
boundaries, membership, 195–196
Briggs, Katharine Cook, 32
Burgo, Joseph, 172
bursty communication, 139–140, 145, 147–148, 215

Cannonball Run, 92
Carter, Jimmy, 1
celebration, 133
Challenger space shuttle, 63–64
change, adapting to, 204–207
chess, 70–71, 73
chickens, 105–107, 120, 121, 123
Christakis, Nicholas, 74
Chrysler, 3
Coach, 202–204
coaching, 73–74, 81
COACH Ways of Working, 202–204
collaboration, 53, 102
common ground, finding, 100–101
communal narcissists, 171–172
communicating in bursts, 139–140, 145, 147–148, 215
community, 111
companies. *See* organizations
competence, 97, 217
competition, 79
Condit, Phil, 189
connection, 94–101, 102, 131, 204–207
contagion, social, 5, 74–75, 79, 80
conversational turn-taking, 140, 150
Corps Franc, 211–212, 217, 220
Covid-19 pandemic, 204
The Creative Curve (Gannett), 73
cult of self, 109–112, 121, 170–171
culture, organizational
  defined, 193–195, 209, 210
  influence, 200, 210
  integration and fulfillment of needs, 200–201, 210
  membership, 195–199, 210
  shared history and values, 201–204, 210
Curie, Marie, 95
Currey, Captain, 215, 218, 220

Daimler-Benz, 3
dark personalities. *See* toxic personalities
Dark Tetrad
  about, 168, 183
  Machiavellianism, 169, 173, 174
  narcissism, 169, 170–172, 174
  psychopathy, 168–169, 170, 174
  sadism, 169, 173, 174
Darth Vader, 63, 64, 65
DARVO behaviors, 172
delusional thinking, 76–77
diamond heist, 153–158, 161–162
Disney, 195
diversity of resources, 159–166
documentation, 177–178
dominant personalities, 21–26
Dream Teams (Snow), 145
Drew, Trafton, 9
Durvasula, Ramani, 174
Dutton, Kevin, 170

Edmondson, Amy, 144
Eisenhower, Dwight D., 90–92, 94, 131, 205
Ellison, Larry, 7
embracing the suck, 76
emotional intelligence, 142–143, 149, 151, 180–181, 183
emotional safety, 196
Enron, 188
Erdős, Anna, 50–51
Erdős, Paul, 50–54, 95
Erdős number, 53
Ericsson, K. Anders, 69–70
Ethiopian Airlines, 191
experts, 6, 9, 27–28, 78, 158

F-16 pilots, 65–67
F-35 pilots, 125–129
failure, 75–77

favor stacking, 98
fear response, 39
Federal-Aid Highway Act (1956), 91
feedback, 79
feelings, as a reason for following a leader, 48–49, 59
Fika tradition, 205
file management, 165, 166
Fong, Christina T., 30
Forer, Bertram, 34
Forer effect, 34–35
Fowler, James, 74
Freston, Tom, 11
Freyd, Jennifer, 172
Friedman, Milton, 187–188, 191

Gallup, 64
Gannett, Allen, 73
Gates, Bill, 54, 70
gender diversity, 141–143, 160–161
general intelligence, 123–124
Get to Know You Bingo, 101
Gladwell, Malcolm, 69
G-LoC (Gravity-induced Loss of Consciousness), 66–67
glue players, 114–115, 119–120, 122, 123, 143, 167, 178–182, 184, 208
goals, alignment of, 126–129, 132–133
Google, 63, 144, 196
grandiose narcissists, 171
Great British Psychopath Survey, 170
Green, Draymond, 61–62, 68–69
Green Belt movement, 55
group selection theory, 107
groupthink, 112
Grove, Andy, 25
growth, 57–58
growth mindset, 78

habits
    attention-creating, 150–151
    contagious, 74–75
    defining team intelligence, 124–125
    stopping bad, 66–68, 82

Hare, Robert D., 170
Hart, William, 39
Harvard Business School (HBS), 26, 27–29
Hawthorne effect, 29
Heath, David, 198
highways, 88–92
history, shared, 201–204, 210
honesty, 97, 217

ideas, 145–146
Ikea effect, 98, 197
inattentional blindness, 9
Indonesian Airlines, 191
Influencers Dinners, 5–6, 75–76
influences, 5, 74–75, 200, 210
information hygiene, 165
intelligence, 3, 123–124. *See also* team intelligence
International Labour Organization, 64
Interstate Highway System, 90–92
Iverson, Allen, 2

James, LeBron, 2, 61, 70, 118, 119
Janis, Irving, 112
Jenner, Kendall, 40
Jobs, Steve, 7, 174–175
Jung, Carl, 31–32

Kahn, Todd, 202–204
Kasparov, Gary, 73
Katzenberg, Jeffrey, 3
Kauffman, Draper L., 211–222
Kellerman, Barbara, 12–13, 27
Kennedy, John F., 219–220
Khan Academy, 2
Knudstorp, Jørgen Vig, 137–138, 139, 143
Kostelnick, Pete, 89
Kraus, Michael W., 94

Larsen, Kaj, 218
leaders and leadership
    alpha mentality, 21–26, 42
    authentic, 36–41, 42

leaders and leadership (*continued*)
   conflicting traits of effective, 4, 7, 54
   connection model, 94–95
   defining, 45–50, 59, 207
   fluidity, 130–131, 133–134
   military, 77–80
   paradox of success, 14–15
   power struggles, 130–131
   star talent narrative, 10–12
   super skills, 54–55, 56–58, 59
   training, 12–13, 26–31, 42, 88, 218
   trickle-down strategy, 86–92, 93
Lee, Justin "Hasard," 125–129
Leegere, John, 198
LEGO, 135–140, 143–144, 145–146, 196
Lewis, Michael, 116
likability, 96, 102
Lincoln, Abraham, 95
Lincoln Highway expedition, 88–90

Maathai, Wangarai Muta, 54–55
Machiavelli, Niccolò, 169
Machiavellianism, 169, 173
Mack, Arien, 9
Macnamara, Brooke, 70
Makogonov, Vladimir, 73
malignant narcissists, 172
managing up, 87
Marvel, 2, 201
Massachusetts Institute of Technology (MIT), 26
Mayo, Elton, 28–29
MBA programs, 26–31, 42
McDonald, Duff, 28
McDonnell Douglas, 188
McKinnell, Hank, 11
McKinsey & Company, 30
McNerney, Jim, 189
Mech, L. David, 22–23
media coverage, 24–25, 42
membership, sense of
   boundaries, 195–196
   common symbol system, 198–199
   creating, 195

   emotional safety, 196
   personal investment, 197–198
   sense of belonging and identification, 196–197
memory, 159
mentorship, 73–74
Merrill Lynch, 11
Microsoft, 54, 70, 127
middle management, 27–28
military
   commander's intent, 127–128
   Kauffman's career in, 211–222
   pilot training, 125–129
   training and development, 77–80, 216–217
mind blindness, 141–142
Missionaries of Charity, 47
mission statements, 127
Moi, Daniel arap, 55
Monitor Consulting, 30
Morey, Daryl, 113–114, 116, 121–122, 123, 143, 161
Moth, 72
Mother Teresa, 46–49
Muir, William, 105–107, 120, 121, 123
multiplier effect, 178–180
Musk, Elon, 7, 54, 55
Myers, Isabel Briggs, 32
Myers-Briggs Type Indicator (MBTI), 32–36
mythology, group, 201–204, 210

narcissism, 169, 170–172, 174
narratives, 40, 201–204, 210
Navy Bomb Disposal School, 216–217
Navy SEALs, 220–221
NBA All-Stars, 1–2, 10, 61, 109
Neanderthals, 85
needs fulfillment, 200–201, 210
Netflix, 2
neural entrainment, 140
Nikitin, Alexander, 73
Nordstrom, 201–202
Notarbartolo, Leonardo, 153–158, 161–162

O'Leary, Michael, 24–25
Olivero, Gerald, 74
Olympics, 1–2, 61, 108, 118
O'Neal, Stan, 11
organizations
   adapting to change, 204–207
   culture, 193–204, 209, 210
   goal alignment within, 126–129,
     132–133
   paradox of competing
     responsibilities, 187, 193
   retain and reinvest model, 110
   shareholder value, 187–193
Ortberg, Kelly, 192
Outliers (Gladwell), 69

Paine, Neil, 119
Patil, Pratibha, 47
Paulhus, Delroy L., 168, 174
Pentland, Alex, 205
Pepsi, 40
perceptions, 50
personality assessments, 31–36, 42
Peter, Laurence J., 87
Peter Principle, 87–88
Pfeffer, Jeffrey, 30
Pfizer, 11
Phillips, Richard, 220
physical contact, 94
pilots, 65–67, 73, 125–129
Pixar, 2
plane crashes, 191
Pohnpei, Micronesia, 44–45
Popovich, Greg, 119
popularity, 95–96
power struggles, 130–131
pratfall effect, 100
Price, Joseph, 178–179
The Prince (Machiavelli), 169
Prinstein, Mitch, 95–96
proactive thinking, 181–182
productivity, 74
Project Aristotle, 144
promotions, 87–88
psychological safety, 63–64, 82,
   144–146, 149–150, 195, 215

psychopathy, 168–169, 170
pumpkin-spicification process, 199

Quibi, 3

racial diversity, 160–161
reasoning
   goal alignment, 125–129, 132–133
   leadership fluidity, 130–131,
     133–134
   in team intelligence, 124, 162,
     207–208, 219
Reichsautobahn, 90
resources
   cataloging, 163–164
   diversity of, 153–166
   in team intelligence, 125, 162,
     208, 219
retain and reinvest company
   model, 110
rewards, 120, 133, 150–151
Riley, Pat, 119
Robertson, David C., 136–137
Rock, Irvin, 9
Ryanair, 24–25, 30

sadism, 169, 173, 174
safety
   emotional, 196
   psychological, 63–64, 82,
     144–146, 149–150, 195, 215
Second Industrial Revolution,
   27–28
seductive narcissists, 172
self-expression, 40–41
sexual harassment, 64
Shakarov, Alexander, 73
shareholder activists, 110
shareholder value, 187–193
skills
   attitude and, 75–77
   developing, 57–58, 69–71
   diversity of, 159–166, 180, 183
   improving, 62–63, 82
   liabilities of misapplied, 56–57
   mastery of, 70

skills (*continued*)
  matching to advantages, 71–73, 82
  mentorship and coaching, 73–74, 81, 82
  social contagion, 74–75, 79, 80
  success and, 103–105
  super, 54–55, 56–58, 59
Snow, Shane, 145
social contagion, 5, 74–75, 79, 80
social contract, 62–63, 65, 81
social sensitivity, 180–181
Something Beautiful for God (film), 47
Southwest Airlines, 199
Spencer, Joel, 54
stacking, 98
Stanford University, 26
star talent narrative, 10–12
Star Wars (film), 63, 64
status
  obsession with, 43–45
  popularity and, 96
Stephens-Davidowitz, Seth, 93–94
strengths, natural, 71–73, 82
student athletes, 107–109
success
  dark personalities and, 173–174
  effective teams and, 123
  paradox of, 14–15
  physical contact and, 94
  sense of belonging and, 93–94, 109
  skill and, 103–105
Sunday scaries, 48
super chickens, 105–107, 120, 121, 123
super skills, 54–55, 56–58, 59, 212–213
Swaab, Roderick I., 103
symbol systems, 198–199

talent
  balance of, 183
  problem of too much, 103–105, 116, 121
  rewarding, 120
  star, 10–12, 178
  success and, 103–105

task interdependence, 104–105
team intelligence
  attention, 125, 135–151, 162, 208, 219
  defined, 3–4
  diversity of skills and, 159–166
  goal alignment, 126–129, 132–133
  habits defining, 124–125
  increasing, 121
  maximizing, 14–15
  number of women on team and, 141–143, 160–161
  reasoning, 124, 125–134, 162, 207–208, 219
  resources, 125, 153–166, 208, 219
team(s)
  chickens, 105–107, 120
  connection and trust among, 94–101, 131, 204–207, 211–212
  diamond heist, 153–158, 161–162
  diversity of skills, 159–166
  effective, 123
  getting them to stick together, 113–120
  glue players, 114–115, 119–120, 122, 123, 143, 167, 178–182, 184, 208
  ideas and, 145–146
  integration of leadership into, 78–79
  internal power struggles, 130–131
  memory, 159
  necessity of, 85–86
  paradox of success, 14–15
  sense of belonging, 93–94
  sense of membership, 195–199
  as smallest unit of effectiveness, 12, 86, 102
  super, 105–109, 116, 213–214
  too-much-talent problem, 103–105, 116, 121
  toxic personalities on, 167–178
  traits of effective, 4
Team USA, 1–2, 10, 108, 109, 118
10,000 hour rule, 70–71

theory of mind, 141–144
T-Mobile, 198–199
too-much-talent problem, 103–105, 116, 121
toxic personalities
    Dark Tetrad, 168–170, 183
    dealing with, 174–178
    Machiavellianism, 169, 173, 174
    narcissism, 169, 170–172, 174
    negative impacts of, 167–168
    psychopathy, 168–169, 170, 174
    sadism, 169, 173, 174
    success and, 173–174
training
    leadership, 12–13, 88, 218
    MBA programs, 26–31, 42
    military, 77–80, 216–217
    pilots, 125–129
transparency, culture of, 177
trickle-down leadership strategy, 86–92
Trounce, Craig, 201–202
Truman, Harry, 90
trust, 96–101, 102, 131, 184, 204–205, 215, 217–218
Turnkey Teams, 206

Uber, 197
Underwater Demolitions Team, 218–220

values
    alignment with, 195
    shared, 201–204, 210
Viacom, 11
violence in the workplace, 64
Virts, Terry, 65–67, 129
Võ, Melissa, 9
Volkswagen, 188
vulnerability loops, 99–100, 205
vulnerable narcissists, 171

Wade, Dwyane, 2, 118
waterfall leadership strategy, 86–92, 93
Weinstein, Bob, 38–39
Weinstein, Harvey, 38–39
Welch, Jack, 25, 192
Wharton School, 26
Whitman, Meg, 3
Wilkens, Lenny, 1
Williams, Serena, 11–12
The Wolf (Mech), 22
Wolfe, Jeremy, 9
wolves, 22–23
Woolley, Anita Williams, 123–124, 130, 131, 139, 141, 159–166
World Cup, 103–104
World War II, 211–222
Wozniak, Steve, 95

Yale University, 26
yam competition, 44–45
You're Invited (Levy), 85–86

Zappos, 195

About the Author

JON LEVY is a behavioral scientist and the *New York Times* bestselling author of *You're Invited*. Renowned for his groundbreaking insights on trust, leadership, and teams, Levy has been sought after as a speaker and consultant by both the Fortune 500 (Microsoft, Google, AB InBev, Samsung, Merck, etc.) and startups.